ENDAU ROMPIN
a malaysian heritage

Published by

MALAYAN NATURE SOCIETY

sponsors

 MALAYAN NATURE SOCIETY
(SELANGOR BRANCH)

PETROLIAM NASIONAL BERHAD
PETRONAS

 SPORTS TOTO MALAYSIA BERHAD

THE CHENG KIM LOKE FOUNDATION

TAN JIEW HOE

FAR EAST OFFSET AND ENGRAVING SDN. BHD.

CITIBANK

HARRISONS MALAYSIAN PLANTATIONS BERHAD

KUMPULAN GUTHRIE SDN. BHD.

SIME DARBY BERHAD

KOMAL SDN. BERHAD

BUKIT KATIL RUBBER ESTATE LTD

THE ATLAS ICE CO. BHD

AYER MOLEK RUBBER CO. BHD

Canada 🍁

THE MALAYAN NATURE SOCIETY

GRATEFULLY ACKNOWLEDGES THE CONTRIBUTION OF THE

CANADIAN HIGH COMMISSION

TOWARDS THE PUBLICATION OF

"ENDAU-ROMPIN – A MALAYSIAN HERITAGE"

contents

Photo: (JD)

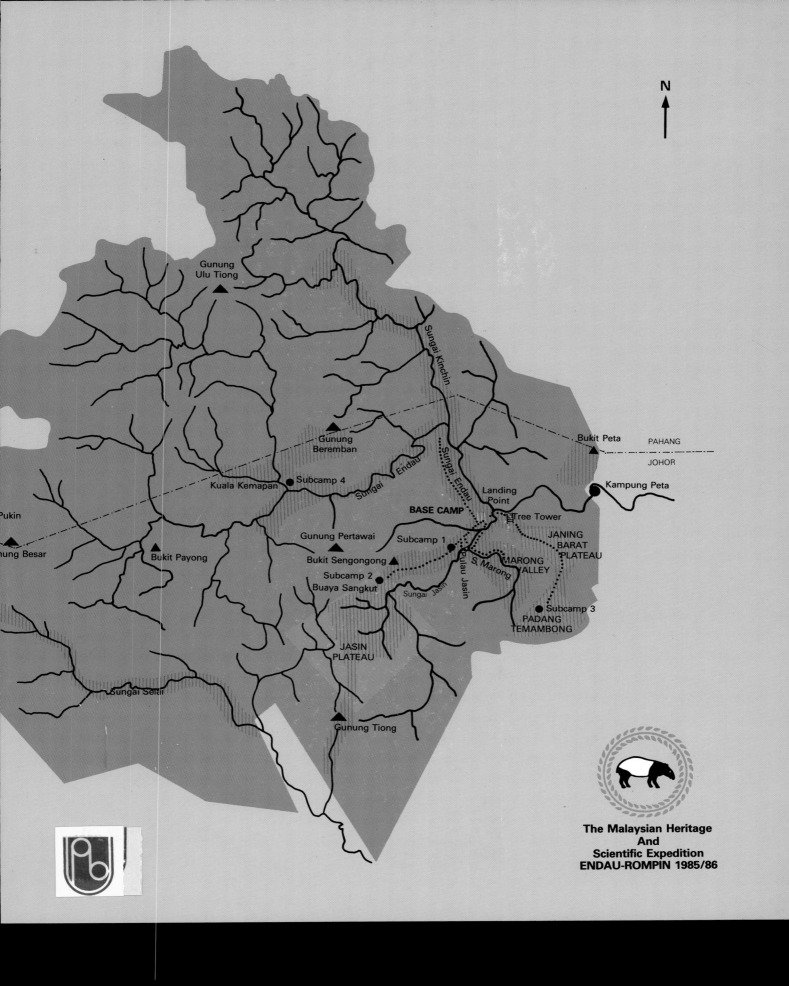

N

Gunung
Ulu Tiong ▲

Sungai Kinchin

Gunung
Beremban ▲

Bukit Peta ▲   PAHANG

                    JOHOR

Kuala Kemapan ● Subcamp 4

Sungai Endau

Sungai Endau

Kampung Peta ●

Landing
Point

BASE CAMP

Tree Tower

Pukin

Gunung Pertawai ▲

Subcamp 1

JANING
BARAT
PLATEAU

nung Besar

Bukit Payong ▲

Bukit Sengongong ▲

Pulau Jasin

S. Marong

MARONG
VALLEY

Subcamp 2 ●
Buaya Sangkut

Sungai Jasin

Subcamp 3 ●
PADANG
TEMAMBONG

JASIN
PLATEAU

Sungai Selai

Gunung Tiong ▲

**The Malaysian Heritage
And
Scientific Expedition
ENDAU-ROMPIN 1985/86**

The Malayan Nature Society is grateful to

Star Publications (Malaysia) Berhad
for their assistance throughout the
Malaysian Heritage and Scientific
Expedition to Endau-Rompin, 1985-1986.

First published 1988
Reprinted 1989

Cataloguing-in-Publication Data
Davison, Geoffrey W.H.
    Endau-Rompin: a Malaysian Heritage/
    Geoffrey W.H. Davison

    1. Endau-Rompin — Natural History
       — Malaysia. I. Title.
    QH 541.5   574.5

ISBN 967-99906-1-3

introduction

Throughout history, Man has been driven by an instinct to explore and discover, to enquire and to improve, to learn and to advance. These instincts, while existing in all peoples irrespective of race and colour, have often not been able to flourish, due to lack of opportunity, training or encouragement.

Malaysians are privileged in that our country, with its luxuriant and diverse natural environment, offers unlimited opportunities for exploration and discovery in natural history. No matter what particular topic of natural history attracts our interest it is possible, through observation and enquiry, to become an expert on that topic, in the country if not in the whole world. Scientific training, if lacking in the past, is now provided by our various institutions of higher learning, while encouragement in the form of public interest and support has never been higher.

The Endau-Rompin Heritage and Scientific Expedition 1985/86 was a real manifestation of the maturity of Malaysian scientists in the field of natural history. This was the first scientific expedition organised by Malaysians in Malaysia for Malaysians. The scientific documentation has been published in the Malayan Nature Journal and is proof of the ability and maturity of the Malaysian scientific community. The scientists have not only discovered new plants, new animals and new ecosystems but more important, the Endau-Rompin Heritage and Scientific Expedition has created an awareness amongst the public of the wealth of our natural history. There still lie within our forests numerous secrets to be discovered and limitless opportunities for Malaysians to pursue scientific endeavours.

The Endau-Rompin Heritage and Scientific Expedition also provided a unique opportunity for hundreds of school children in Malaysia to be brought in and exposed to the wealth, diversity, beauty and grandeur of the Malaysian forests. The children have enjoyed themselves, as was so well documented in the expedition logbook and camp diaries. They have appealed to the authorities to ensure that Endau-Rompin will be conserved in perpetuity and they have been left, in their own words, "richer by this experience."

The Malayan Nature Society is proud to have had the unique privilege of organising this expedition, but it could not have been done without the tremendous and spontaneous support of a host of individuals and institutions who contributed financially and in kind. The public came to the support of MNS in this endeavour under the patronage of our Father of Malaysia, YTM Tunku Abdul Rahman Putra Al-Haj. I would like to take this opportunity to thank YTM Tunku and all the institutions and individual members of the public for the support that made this expedition possible.

I would like to thank all the scientists and MNS members who have committed their time and effort to ensure the success of this expedition. Without their contribution, I am sure we could not have achieved what we did.

To those who did not have the privilege of visiting Endau-Rompin and participating in this expedition, this book may convey an idea of what Endau-Rompin is all about. We would like you readers to enjoy this book and also to take it upon yourselves to support conservation, particularly of the last remaining tropical forests of the country.

I wish you happy reading and hope that this book in some way will inspire future endeavours and serve as a reminder to all of us of our responsibility to ensure the survival of our natural environment.

Dr. Salleh Mohd. Nor
President
MALAYAN NATURE SOCIETY

foreword

In June 1985 I was able to flag off the first group of scientists on their way to Endau-Rompin. The expedition which thus began was a Malaysian effort to explore the hidden treasures of a little known but biologically important part of our beautiful country.

Today we hear more and more of the constant incursions being made into our forest preserve — our natural environment. Our forests are being cut down and opened up for logging and agriculture. As a result of this, opportunities for enjoyment as well as study are diminishing.

Our youth, with varieties of interest to occupy their minds in this modern world, apart from the attractions offered them, look to nature to satisfy their curiosity and to venture into the secrets of nature. It is therefore important to preserve our unexplored treasures in the interest of Malaysian National Heritage. To this end, the Malayan Nature Society included scientists, school pupils, youth groups and university students, and many members of the Malaysian public in the Malaysian Heritage and Scientific Expedition to Endau-Rompin. I am happy, as patron of the expedition and the society, to have been closely associated with such a broad communal enterprise.

The success of the Expedition can be measured by looking through the pages of this book. Plants and animals new to science were discovered. Unique forest types were found on the isolated hills. Magnificent waterfalls added grandeur to the landscapes within which the scientists carried out their studies. Through the photographs published here, even those who have never ventured inside the forest can appreciate a part of our wonderful Malaysian heritage.

It is my pleasure to offer my heartiest congratulations to those who have pioneered this expedition and have produced the book for the benefit of our people.

YTM Tunku Abdul Rahman Putra Al-Haj

the
ENDEAVOUR

the endeavour

The Malaysian Heritage and Scientific Expedition Endau-Rompin 1985-86 marked an important milestone in Malaysia's conservation history. The expedition was the first of its kind to be organised on such a large scale by Malaysians. True there had been others in the past, but they were organised by foreign scientists and the specimens taken away and the results published overseas.

Behind this expedition lay the Malayan Nature Society (MNS), Malaysia's oldest scientific society with a strong membership of scientists and enthusiastic nature lovers. The Star and the Utusan Malaysia, the English-language and Malay-language dailies, gave their co-operation and support.

No funds existed to organise such an expedition. But MNS president Dr Salleh Mohamed Nor, also director of the Forest Research Institute of Malaysia, said: It must be done, no matter what. The MNS Council agreed. We must move the nation in the cause of conservation.

The most effective way to do this would be to involve more people in the conservation of our natural heritage, so rapidly being destroyed. However, the public had first to appreciate its beauty and importance. An expedition into one of our forests, organised on a national scale, would capture the imagination of the people, the Council felt. An expedition of this sort would not only allow Malaysian scientists to delve into the mysteries of the tropical rain forests but also involve the people in every aspect of the endeavour. Thus it was decided that the expedition should be called the Malaysian Heritage and Scientific Expedition.

Various areas in Peninsular Malaysia were suggested for the expedition but the Endau-Rompin rain forest, straddling the border of the states of

Above: Boats at Kampung Peta wait to take the expedition participants upstream. **(A/ME)**
Right: An overview of the expedition area. **(TV3)**

Previous page
Main: Wreathed hornbills
Rhyticeros undulatus. **(MS)**
Inset, left: Expedition vehicles enter Endau-Rompin. **(HHH)**
Inset, right: The sandstone cliff on Gunung Janing Barat was a challenge for adventurous school children. **(KR)**

Pahang Darul Makmur and Johor Darul Takzim, was unanimously chosen because:

- The area is one of the few remaining expanses of lowland rain forest left in Peninsular Malaysia.

- Lowland tropical rain forest is renowned throughout the world for its richness in species and complexity in structure. The majority of Malaysia's mammals, birds and other animals are found in the lowland forest, of which Endau-Rompin is one of the most southerly in continental Asia.

- The area has been poorly explored and is scientifically little known.

- It is under great pressure from logging, and species in danger of becoming extinct there include the Sumatran rhinoceros *Dicerorhinus sumatrensis*.

- In the Third Malaysia Plan of 1976-1980, it was proposed that the area be gazetted as a second national park. Scientific information obtained through the expedition could help the authorities in making this a reality.

Numerous discussions were held to identify a suitable site to set up base camp, to develop a programme for the expedition and to thrash out the logistics of such a massive endeavour. At the same time, plans were drawn up to raise funds not only from business organisations but, more important, from the public. Six months later, with no full-time professional staff to canvass for funds or to run the expedition, and with great trepidation the Council officially announced its decision to organise the expedition.

A joint MNS-Star co-ordinating committee, responsible for the overall organisation of the expedition, was set up. In addition, a technical committee was convened to direct and co-ordinate the scientific and educational aspects of the expedition.

The Expedition Gets Under Way

Official permission to carry out the expedition in Endau-Rompin was obtained from the Pahang and Johor governments. On April 30, 1985, herpetologist Dr Kiew Bong Heang, who had been appointed expedition leader, took a small party on a reconnaissance trip to select the site for base camp. The place chosen was at Kuala Jasin, the confluence of Sungai Jasin and Sungai Endau and about an hour's boat ride from Kampung Peta. This village is inhabited by Orang Hulu, aboriginals or indigenous people, and with their help a sleeping hut, kitchen and a small store were built at Kuala Jasin.

All was set then for the launch. On June 2, 1985, the nation's first Prime Minister, Tunku Abdul Rahman Putra Al-Haj, who had consented to be patron of the expedition, flagged off a convoy of three vehicles from his house at Jalan Tunku in Kuala Lumpur.

So the Endau-Rompin expedition began — with little more than faith, energy, determination, $10,000 from the society's own meagre resources and a few promises. Fortunately, response to appeals for funds was quick and encouraging. Contributions in cash and kind poured in. As news of the expedition spread, the people dipped into their pockets and came out with donations big and small. Firms did the same. Fund-raising drives were organised. The result — about $250,000 was eventually raised. Although this was nowhere near the estimated cost of $433,000, it was enough, for the budget had been trimmed to cover the bare essentials. Donations of canned food, toiletries and hardware were useful while the loan of four-wheel drive vehicles helped cut costs.

Above: Black-and-Yellow Broadbill
Eurylaimus ochromalus. (MS)
Left: Female Sumatran rhinoceros
Dicerorhinus sumatrensis.
(*TMNY)
Far left: Young frond of **Matonia
pectinata** at Padang Temambong.
(SLG)

Top: Expedition patron Tunku Abdul Rahman Putra Al-Haj flags off the first convoy from his residence in Kuala Lumpur.
Above: Datuk Shahrir bin Abdul Samad, then Federal Territory Minister, boosted expedition morale with his visit. (TYP)

By the end of November 1985, about 500 people had visited the expedition area. They included students, school children, and members of the public, many of them coming as volunteers.

The base camp area was a hive of activity with scientists conducting both long term and short term experiments. Collecting forays into the forest for plants, fungi, animals, soil and rocks were the preoccupation of many scientists. Geologists and soil scientists were keen to unravel the geological events of time past. Volunteers were encouraged to assist scientists and help in the daily chores of the camp. Universities sent students to acquaint them with field research techniques. School students participated in a formal nature programme to introduce them to the structure and functioning of the forest. All participants of course had ample time to enjoy the scenic beauty of the forest, its crystal clear rivers and waterfalls.

A number of cross-country sub-expeditions were organised. Some of these adventures are recorded in Chapter 4. A major sub-expedition took a party of 14 across Endau-Rompin in 10 days in March 1986. The tough hike was to take the party from the Gunung Besar area over to the headwaters of Sungai Endau and down to Kuala Jasin and base camp, but the party followed the wrong stream and ended up going down Sungai Selai instead! However, the journey proved to be scientifically worthwhile, because a new species of *Didissandra,* an attractive flowering herb endemic to the river valley, was discovered.

The expedition was to end in December 1985, but by then the Council had decided to extend it by another six months. There were two reasons: long term experiments would be more meaningful if data

Above: Hundreds of school children were introduced to forest ecology during the expedition. (TYP)
Far left: Major assistance was received from the people of Kampung Peta. (A/ME)
Left: Even seemingly featureless rocks held secrets for geologists. (TV3)

Above: Growth of clubmoss **Lycopodium phlegmaria** *is tipped by the branching fertile fronds.* (KR)
Left: Pitcher plant **Nepenthes ampullaria.** (KR)
Right: Tree roots zigzag up trunks of the new fan palm **Livistona endauensis.** (KR)
Far right: On Gunung Janing Barat a third of all trees were fan palms. (YPK)

were collected over a full annual cycle, and many more people would be able to participate.

The Endau-Rompin area

The expedition area lies at the headwaters of Sungai Endau astride the Johor-Pahang border. It covers an area of 870 square kilometres, about one and a half times the size of Singapore island. It includes parts of the Labis and Endau-Mas forest reserves in Johor and the Lesong Forest Reserve in Pahang. These forest reserves cover a contiguous area of hilly sandstone-capped country, which is traditionally used by the Jakun or Orang Hulu people of northern Johor.

The area contains a unique assemblage of tropical lowland and hill rain forest with pristine rivers and varied wildlife. The vegetation has some affinity to that of the coastal parts of Sarawak, besides possessing its own plants found nowhere else in the world. This botanical distinctiveness is further enhanced by the presence of open bog-like vegetation on top of the various hills, ridges and plateaux in the area. It is also home to the

Top: Butterflies, common and rare, were the subject of a special study. **(A/ME)**
Above: Yellow polka dots may be a warning to stay away. **(A/ME)**
Left: Immature Wagler's Pit-viper **Trimeresurus wagleri.** **(PG)**

Above: Jeram Upeh Guling, attractive to geologists as well as swimmers. **(MK)**

largest Malaysian population of that highly endangered animal, the Sumatran rhinoceros. This makes the area an important part of Malaysia's natural heritage that is badly in need of conservation.

The very first visit to Endau-Rompin for scientific purposes was in 1892, when miner and surveyor H.W. Lake and Lieutenant H.J. Kelsall climbed Gunung Janing. At the eastern end of the hill they determined the altitude of its highest point, fixed its position by triangulation on neighbouring peaks, and collected plant specimens. During this journey, they were able to record a number of the more striking animals, such as elephants, monkeys and hornbills. In 1933 the Endau-Kluang Wildlife Reserve was gazetted, to help protect some of these animals, bringing the area within the interest of the Game Department. Then in 1972 the Pahang

Tenggara Development Authority earmarked part of Endau-Rompin, the part within the Lesong Forest Reserve in Pahang, as a nature reserve free from development. An Endau-Rompin Management Plan was drafted by the Department of Wildlife and National Parks, and representations were made to the Pahang and Johor state governments in the hope that they would make it a national park. Despite the fact that it had been identified in the 1976-1980 Third Malaysia Plan as a future national park, controversy raged over continued logging. The Malayan Nature Society's interest in Endau-Rompin dates back to before 1970, with descriptions of the area's vegetation in the society's journal. It continued through the peak of the 1977 logging controversy and has been strengthened by the Heritage and Scientific Expedition.

The objectives
The expedition's objectives were to:

- document all species of plants and animals encountered in the area, focusing on rare and endemic species.

- study the geology, limnology and climatology of the area.

- provide scientific reports that would be readily available to government agencies, students and the public.

- involve Malaysians in the expedition so that they might experience and appreciate our natural heritage.

The year-long expedition has to a large extent achieved its objectives. More than 70 scientists from diverse disciplines participated in the expedition. More important, it has made Malaysians aware of Endau-Rompin. The fact that the state governments of Johor and Pahang are now setting up separate state parks in the Endau-Rompin area can · be attributed largely to this effort.

Above: A caterpillar's head, made fantastic in close-up. (A/ME)
Left: Glandular frog **Rana glandulosa** (PG)

LANDSCAPES
of endau-rompin

landscapes of endau~rompin

Previous page
Main: *Ignimbrite at Kuala Jasin, key to Endau-Rompin's past.* **(KSN)**
Inset, top: *Falls on the Sungai Lemakoh.* **(RA)**
Inset, bottom: *Buaya Sangkut waterfalls.* **(TV3)**

Below: *Many hills, like Gunung Beremban, were topped by sandstone plateaux.* **(SLG)**
Right: *The rocky bed of the upper Sungai Endau.* **(HHH)**

The Endau-Rompin area is endowed with a variety of natural features — hills, rocks, cliffs and waterfalls — all of which add to the attractiveness of the landscape. To the geologist, they reveal a very ancient history.

The hills of Endau-Rompin stand out in isolation from the surrounding level ground of Pahang and Johor, forming a single, compact and very rugged unit. Ignimbrite, a volcanic rock, is the main material from which these hills are made, overlain in places by thinner layers of shale and sandstone.

Volcanic Crystals

Quartz crystal ignimbrite can be seen on the surface at many points: at the rapids on the Sungai Endau, at the expedition base camp, on the upper parts of Jeram Upeh Guling, and in waterfalls along the slopes of hills like Gunung Janing and Gunung Beremban. Along the old logging roads ignimbrite has been decomposed by weathering to form sharp-edged chips, often with a pale "skin" on their surfaces.

A piece of ignimbrite, say a river cobble from the bridge below the base camp, shows several interesting textures. Its most characteristic feature is the presence of quartz crystals, rounded glassy-looking particles

Carboniferous – Lower Permian

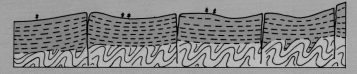

Lower – Mid. Permian

Mid. Permian – Triassic

Upper Triassic

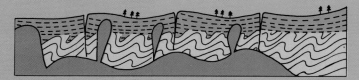

Jurassic

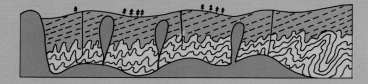

Upper Jurassic – Lower Cretaceous

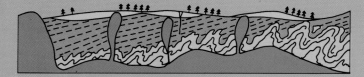

Present Day

Geology in brief

The earliest known history of the Ulu Endau involved massive, violent volcanic outpourings. These were in the form of ash, and were on a scale comparable with the more recent eruptions around Lake Toba, Sumatra. As a result great volumes of ignimbrite were deposited, in places 900 metres thick.

The Jurassic period, 150 million years ago, when apparently more rocks were being worn away than created, has left its mark in Endau-Rompin mainly as a gap in the story.

Then, during the Cretaceous, a sequence of sandstone and shale was deposited. The geological and biological features of the landscape were possibly not unlike the modern-day Endau region, though dinosaurs and pterodactyls would have been seen instead of elephants and eagles.

Since then, extensive erosion has cut into the ignimbrite, and has reduced the sandstone to a few remnants capping the hills and mountains.

	Ignimbrite		Granitic Intrusion
	Metasediments		Sandstone

Fossil wood of the pine *Araucarioxylon* indicates rocks of Upper Triassic age. (IM)

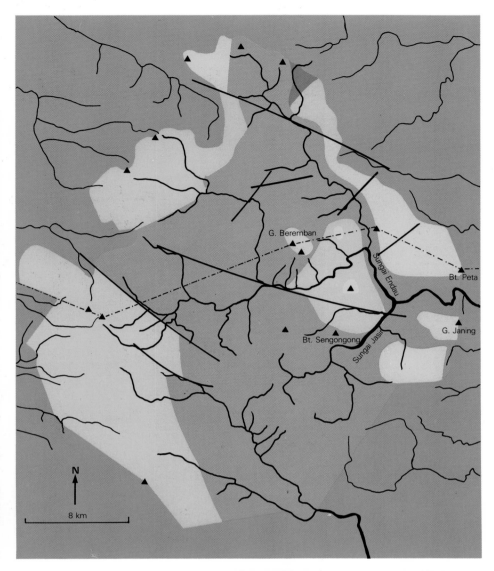

Map legend:

Tebak Formation
Sandstone shale and
Siltstone

Mersing Beds
Phyllites, schist and
slate

Granite
Biotite Adamellite and
Hornfels

Jasin Volcanics
Acid Pyroclastics

Fault

Map labels: G. Beremban, Bt. Peta, Sungai Endau, G. Janing, Bt. Sengongong, Sungai Jasin, N, 8 km

*With the years, even rivers have
changed their course, as at Kuala
Marong.* **(KSN)**

embedded in the stone. Sometimes it is possible to see black streaks an inch or so long, compressed pumice, or even little splinters of welded glass. Often the ignimbrite of Endau-Rompin contains within itself ignimbrite fragments of even greater age, swallowed up by slightly younger rock, showing that the same process of rock formation has occurred more than once.

Ignimbrite has a spectacular genesis. It is volcanic, as the black streaks of pumice show. But it is not formed from lava. The mechanism of its formation is known to geologists as "ash flow eruption". This is the most violent type of volcanic convulsion: a small ash flow early in this century destroyed a city of 30,000 people in Martinique, West Indies, within a few minutes. During an ash flow eruption, such as deposited the rock at base camp, or on the slopes of Gunung Janing, there was a huge release of hot gas from within the earth. At perhaps 1000 degrees centigrade, the gas carried with it sand-sized crystals of quartz and shards of glass, fragments of pumice and larger pieces of pre-existing rock. Such clouds of ash can travel at speeds of up to 100 kilometres an hour. Eventually the heavier particles would begin to settle, often retaining enough heat to weld themselves together.

The ash clouds producing the great volume of Endau-Rompin ignimbrite were probably emitted from many cracks and fissures in the earth, rather than a single, conical volcano. A series of repeated eruptions would have gradually built up an extensive plateau of rocks.

It is very unlikely that such a deposit could have formed under water. When the Endau ignimbrite was formed, therefore, this region was already dry land, not beneath the sea. Another line of thinking, suggested by geologists during the expedi-

LANDSCAPES OF ENDAU-ROMPIN 27

tion, arose from the fact that big ignimbrite deposits are confined to particular regions of the world. Usually, as in Sumatra, these are places where the surface crust of the earth is being subsumed in deep ocean trenches. One section or plate of the earth's surface is pushed gradually beneath another, and returns to the molten interior. This creates a lot of volcanic activity, as at Lake Toba in the past and many other Sumatran volcanos today. Two hundred million years ago, ask the geologists, was the future Endau-Rompin close to the edge of such a moving plate?

Enormous forces must have been experienced by rocks pressing against one another, causing faults and crack-lines which can be seen today. Where igneous rocks like granite have been squeezed, they have often fractured, the crack-lines crossing each other at angles of about 60 degrees. Why the angle is always the same is complex physics, but this 60 degree angle can be seen everywhere, at Buaya Sangkut, at Padang Temambong and at Jeram Upeh Guling.

Sand and Clay

Seen from a distance, from a boat on the Sungai Endau, or when driving in from Rompin, the flat-topped hills of the expedition area are characteristic. They remind one of the scenery in a cowboy movie. On these flat plateaux a sequence of sandstone and shale is exposed, for instance on the upper part of Gunung Janing and on Padang Temambong. A very thin remnant, about three metres thick, lies on the top of Gunung Beremban. At its edges, the sandstone commonly forms cliffs, and a line of cliffs can be seen all along the side of Gunung Janing, marked by a change in the covering vegetation. When walking uphill through the forest, this cliff forms a barrier which must be climbed, and lumps of soft sandstone are

Below: Bare soil on logging tracks is vulnerable to rapid erosion. **(MK)**

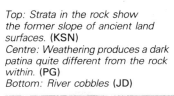

Top: Strata in the rock show the former slope of ancient land surfaces. **(KSN)**
Centre: Weathering produces a dark patina quite different from the rock within. **(PG)**
Bottom: River cobbles **(JD)**

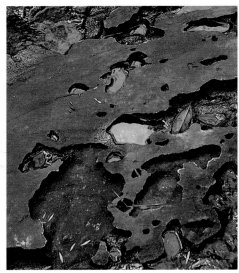

Above: The fairy tale atmosphere of Padang Temambong. (**SLG**)
Right: A skin of weathered sandstone has patchily survived the continual action of the water. (**GD**)
Far right: The cliff of Gunung Janing, a foothold for herbs. (**JD**)

Animal trails and a wallow on Padang Temambong are distinct enough to be seen from the air. **(TV3)**

likely to break off and roll downhill. This sandstone is simply a rock formed of sand particles, almost entirely quartz in composition, pressed very hard together.

Over such layered cliffs water of the swollen streams falls in stepped cascades. A good example was found just downstream of the sub-camp at Padang Temambong, where an almost fairy-tale atmosphere is created by the sparkling water edged by delicate ferns.

The shale does not normally occur in outcrops, and its presence must be inferred from the deposits of whitish clay which are found on Gunung Janing and Padang Temam-

bong. There, the sticky clay has been used as a wallow by wild pigs. Both these places are often waterlogged.

A sequence of sandstone and shale could have been deposited in one of several different ways, but it is commonly accepted that the Endau-Rompin sandstone was laid down by the action of rivers. Any of the large, modern day rivers (including the lower Endau) would make a good analogue. Sand is deposited in the river bed and in sand bars; clay is deposited when the river overflows its banks during floods. Over long periods of time a river system may wander laterally and produce extensive deposits. Once again the action of

Above: Huge boulders can be tumbled about like pebbles when the river is in flood. (TS)
Right: Rheophytes, plants resistant to floods, typically have slender leaves and tough stems. (WKM)
Far right: Buaya Sangkut waterfall was the most spectacular expedition discovery. (SLG)

Plants struggle for a foothold in crevices where they can obtain a few nutrients. **(KSN)**

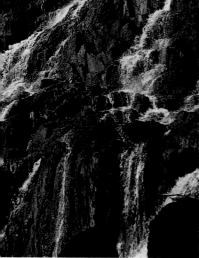

rivers, in depositing the raw materials for sandstone, is evidence that the area was dry land, not in a maritime environment.

The third rock type which contributes to the landscapes of Endau-Rompin is granite. It is a plutonic rock, produced by the underground cooling and solidification of molten rock. The size of the crystals in the rock is a guide to the rate of cooling, which is slower the deeper underground the rock was formed. Here, the granite must have cooled several kilometres underneath the earth's surface. Now, it can be seen at the surface at one spot not too far from base camp, in the lower stretches of Jeram Upeh Guling. It contains varied crystals of quartz and feldspar, hornblende and biotite, fragments which, when seen under the magnifying glass, are as beautiful as their names.

Ancient Life

Relatively few fossils have been found in Endau-Rompin, and expedition geologists failed in their ambition to locate the remains of ancient backboned animals. The place to search was in the sandstone caps of hills such as Gunung Beremban, but there the area of exposed rock was small and no animal fossils were found. Ancient plants, however, are known from the shales of Bukit Peta and Gunung Janing: *Ptilophyllum pterophylloides* and *Gleichenoides pantiensis* are two of these. Another four or five plants, all of similar age, about 140 million years old, have been found within the general area of Ulu Endau by previous explorers, and these plants form part of a flora which must once have been widely distributed over the eastern half of the peninsula.

One fossil found by good luck during the expedition was a piece of fossilised wood, lying on the surface. Thin sections of this fossil still show

Right: A paradox, that such a futuristic landscape should be the product of millions of years past. **(KSN)**

Below: Rushing waters show how the adjacent rock can be eroded. **(KSN)**

Below right: The bath-tubs of Sungai Jasin. **(KSN)**

the fine details of its cells, and allow it to be identified as a species of conifer, now extinct.

At least some of the geological data suggest that the sandstone sediments, which now cap the hill tops, were formed in a relatively dry and warm climate. This seems to agree with the kinds of plants preserved in the fossil record — ferns, cycads and conifers. Few species of plants have been preserved, but they are relatives of modern plants which today live in warm and open habitats.

The Power of the Water

Events many millions of years ago still have major effects upon the region and its wildlife. Each of the major rivers, the Endau, the Selai and the Jasin, is marked by waterfalls. At the 40 metre Buaya Sangkut waterfalls, water spills down from a languid reach of pools into a tumble of rugged boulders. Waterfalls like this show the observant visitor where different layers of rock meet one another; over long periods the action of the water slowly eats away

the softer rock while harder rock remains. At some of the larger falls, too, bands of granite may have slipped against one another where they meet, to form a step down which the water tumbles.

At Jeram Upeh Guling, round "bath-tubs" can be found near the top of the falls, ground out of the solid rock. Perhaps, millions of years ago, a little pebble lodged in a crevice and was spun round and round by the flowing water. Gradually this spinning pebble would have worn

away a larger hole for itself, a hole which trapped larger stones brought down river by the next flood. So the process would have gone on, till today we see boulders lying within a hole, perhaps a metre or so across and maybe two metres deep. Water-worn pebbles form most of the river beds. Sungai Jasin for instance, is stony for nearly all its length. In places the pebbles have built up to form raised beds which are now scoured only by the more extreme floods, and where shrubs and weeds have gained a foothold.

Much greater forces must have been involved in tumbling the rugged rocks of the major waterfalls. With about 80 cubic metres of water (17,000 gallons) flowing over Buaya Sangkut every second, then continuing down to Jeram Upeh Guling and beyond, even huge boulders can be thrown about like pebbles. At the water's edge small plants may find a home, but an unsafe one, amongst the boulders. Where the water flows parallel to the exposed layers of uptilted rock, lines of stone protrude from the river. Gradually the channels between them will be deepened.

During the expedition, scientists reported very low concentrations of minerals such as calcium, iron and magnesium in the river water. All three rock types of the area, ignimbrite, sandstone and granite, have low content of such minerals, and so the geology of Endau-Rompin is likely to affect today the kinds and numbers of animals living in the water.

On Gunung Janing, water and stone interact in a different way. The shales and clay on the plateau are impermeable to water, so part of the hill top is permanently damp underfoot. The ground is poor in nutrients and, because of water-logging, what nutrients exist are

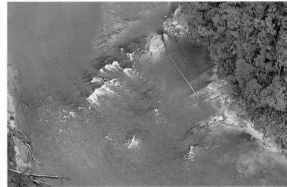

Above: A different perspective: the river acts on rocks, sand and tree. **(TMNY)**
Far left: Below Buaya Sangkut falls, water rushes past the jagged rocks. **(PG)**
Left: Pebble beaches of the Sungai Jasin contrast with the rapids and waterfalls elsewhere. **(YPK)**

Above: Pulau Jasin, an hour from Base Camp, formed a focus for many studies. **(MK)**

The many faces of Pulau Jasin, where ferns and stunted trees manage to survive among the flood-prone rocks.

(YPK)

(KSN)

(KR)

difficult for plants to obtain. Pitcher plants have solved the problem by eating insects. The little climbing *Dischidia* provides a home for ants in its pitcher-shaped leaves, and the ants carry debris and nutrients to the plants.

One of the few islands in the Jasin river, Pulau Jasin, an hour's walk from camp is washed yearly by high water. Its vegetation is stunted and gnarled. *Leptospermum* trees, typically fond of mountain tops, here grow less than 50 metres above sea level, in company with the fern *Dipteris conjugata* and many orchids. The island itself consists of river boulders, amongst which sand has been trapped by the plants' roots. Every so often plants, and even sections of the island itself, are pulled away by floods. The result is a nutrient-poor environment, with sand to grow in but little organic matter in the soil, and an environment which is physically unstable.

Weather and water have combined in Padang Temambong to create curious patterns on exposed rocks. Where the sandstone is exposed in the stream bed, the rock surface has been hardened by sunlight, heat, and perhaps by the growth of algae. But beneath this hard skin the sandstone is softer, and has been worn away by the stream. This has left, in places, a tough but slender tracery of surface rock, under which runs a labyrinth of little holes and tunnels.

In both big and small ways, therefore, the landscape of Endau-Rompin is the product of many different forces. It depends upon the age and the type of rocks. It depends on the course of the rivers and the nutrients they carry with them. It depends upon the gradual action of their waters, a force which will continue to act in subtly changing ways as time goes by.

into the
FOREST

into the forest

The tallest tree ever measured in a Malaysian forest was a tualang *Koompassia excelsa*. It stood a proud 84 m tall. Individual trees approaching this record can be found in many forests, including Endau-Rompin.

The great height to which some of these forest giants soar makes it difficult for earthbound man to view the forest as a whole. To give access to the forest canopy at Endau-Rompin, an engineering unit of the Malaysian armed forces constructed a 10-storey wooden tower. It was built around a particularly straight and tall keruing tree, *Dipterocarpus costulatus,* reaching to the topmost twigs where the expedition flag later flew. From the top level, scientists and visitors were free to look monkeys, birds and squirrels in the eye.

Beyond the sea of ruffled tree crowns lay the entire Endau and Jasin river valleys, the region where much of the expedition's work was concentrated. Characteristic of this area were the steep sandstone-capped ridges, which were to reveal some of the expedition's more spectacular finds.

Canopy Of Trees

The uniform muted greens of the tree canopy conceal the rich diversity of tree species of which the forest is

Far left/Left: The tree tower, built
around a keruing kipas tree **Dipterocarpus costulatus,** has ten
platforms at 3-metre intervals, for
work at different levels in the forest.
(HHH) (DL)
Above: From halfway up the tower
the visitor can look out at the crowns
of the smaller trees and palms. (MS)

Previous page
Main: Orchid **Dendrobium
revolutum.** (JD)
Inset, left: **Selaginella intermedia.**
(A/ME)
Inset, right: Yellow breasted
flowerpecker **Prionochilus
maculatus** (MS)

Above: Freshly sprouting leaves of the keruing kipas are close enough for the climber to touch by leaning from the tower. **(LC)**
*Right: Seraya **Shorea curtisii.*** **(KR)**

composed. Some 2,500 tree species have been recorded from Peninsular Malaysia, and frequently there are more than 100 species in a single hectare. The lowland forest around the tree tower was typical of this diversity, with keruing, *Dipterocarpus* spp. and meranti, *Shorea* spp., kapur, *Dryobalonops* spp., rengas, *Gluta* spp. and a host of other big trees. Plots were marked out to count this diversity on Gunung Janing Barat.

The uneven green layer of the forest canopy is like a surface skin, beneath which the branches and trunks form a supporting skeleton. Many groups of forest-living animals are confined to this upper layer, for it is within the growing trees that much of the forest's nutrients are stored.

Hornbills are one such group. Being large birds, they can cover great distances every day to feed on fruits, carefully selected for their type and ripeness, from amongst those available on the tree tops. Seven species were found at Endau, wreathed and rhinoceros hornbills the commonest amongst them.

Though all are found together, each has a distinct place within the economy of nature. Pied hornbills, *Anthracoceros albirostris,* the smallest, are typical of the forest edge, and live along the Sungai Endau. Rhinoceros and helmeted hornbills, *Buceros rhinoceros* and *Rhinoplax vigil,* the very biggest, hardly ever move below the tree canopy, and need particularly big hollow trees for nesting. The smaller species can pluck fruits from nearer the tips of branches, whilst the heavier birds must find more secure perches from which to feed.

For the famous Rajah Brooke birdwing butterfly, *Trogonoptera brookiana* the canopy plays an especially intriguing role. While males are reasonably common low down along forest streams, females seem to pre-

(MG)

fer higher, hillier country, where they live up in the forest canopy seeking nectar from the flowers of trees and creepers.

The female butterflies seem to fly later in the evening than the males, but both sexes have been found together in the early morning: perhaps it is then that mating occurs. The Rajah Brooke birdwings at Endau proved to be of a special east coast variety, known also from Pahang and Terengganu, in which the males and females are less distinct than elsewhere both in looks and behaviour.

There are probably thousands of insect varieties found only in the forest canopy. In South America, recent work on insects in the tree tops has suggested there might be as many as 15 million species worldwide, rather than the three million assumed earlier. Work in the canopy is physically difficult. The tree tower at Endau-Rompin made it possible to set up light-traps there for the study of moths. Identification of the catch is a major task, and amongst the hundreds of moths, there are undoubtedly several species new to science.

One of the local troops of dusky leaf monkeys, *Presbytis obscura* occupied the area around the tree tower on Gunung Janing Barat. Their presence could be detected by the movement of branches and by the male's extraordinary braying call, but they were nevertheless not easy to see. Most of their food, leaves with a selection of flowers and fruit, was derived from the canopy, and a large part of their day was spent eating. These monkeys can almost be thought of as tree-living cows, for like cows their stomachs are divided into sections where their vegetable food is fermented by bacteria. Leaves are the one item in great supply throughout the forest, so one might well wonder why there aren't groups of monkeys in every tree. Only a small

Top left: The smaller southern pied hornbill **Anthracoceros albirostris** *is found along rivers in tangled growth and sunny spots amongst low trees.* **(KR)**
Top right: High in the canopy over base camp, a rhinoceros hornbill **Buceros rhinoceros** *keeps watch. Its red eye identifies this as a male; females have white eyes.* **(MS)**
Below left: The bushy-crested hornbill **Anorrhinus galeritus** *makes up for its drab colouring by the noisy laughter and chattering by which individuals in a flock maintain contact.* **(MS)**

Above: White-handed gibbons **Hylobates lar** *are totally dependent upon the trees for food and habitat.* **(*MK)**

Below right: Dusky leaf-monkeys **Presbytis obscura** **(MS)**

proportion of the leaves are in fact suitable food; many others contain latex, tannins, phenols and other chemicals, any one of which can kill the monkey's intestinal bacteria and leave it with a stomachful of indigestible leaves.

The white-handed gibbons, *Hylobates lar* also live in the tree tops. Their whooping calls resound between the hills. But unlike the gangs of leaf monkeys, the gentler gibbons live in faithful pairs with their children. While sitting in base camp it was possible to pick out the different families, not only by their position but also by their calls. Each female gave a characteristic number of notes, always five, or six, or seven, and in one family, mother and daughter often gave a spectacular joint performance.

Not all the plants in the forest canopy are tall trees; two other types of plants, lianes and epiphytes, are also found there.

Lianes are tall, woody-stemmed climbers, whose large crowns are carried up to the canopy with the growth of their supporting tree. In a sense they are being stretched between the ever-rising tree and the ground dropping away beneath. One of these climbers bore huge fruits, which were later found to be used in a most surprising way (Chapter 5).

Epiphytes are usually small herbaceous plants that get sufficient light by sitting on the branches of trees, though without gaining any nutrients from them. All their nutrients come from rain water, or from dead leaves and debris which may be trapped around their roots. At Endau-Rompin a conspicuously massive epiphyte is the pandan, *Pandanus epiphyticus,* which in Peninsular Malaysia is found only in Johor.

The vast majority of epiphytes in Malaysia are either orchids or ferns. Both have extremely tiny propagules – the seeds of orchids and the spores of ferns – which, like dust, are light enough to be carried by the wind.

Over 1,000 species of orchids are to be found in Peninsular Malaysia, and special attention was paid to this group of plants by scientists in Endau-Rompin. Perhaps one day new varieties will be cultivated as a result.

Living not on the branches but on the leaves of trees and under-storey plants, epiphylls are minute epiphytes – lichens, alga and bryophytes – using the other plant mainly as a platform on which to grow. They are only found in the forests. Some extract nutrients from the rainwater and any dust which settles on them, while others fix nitrogen from the air, and still others are partially parasitic!

Top: **Bulbophyllum vaginatum,** *an epiphytic orchid at Buaya Sangkut.* **(SLG)**
Above: **Pandanus epiphyticus** *is one of the largest epiphytes, and provides a link between the flora of Johor and Borneo.* **(SLG)**
Right: The purple-leaved **Oberonia anceps** *is an epiphytic orchid about 10 cm across.* **(RA)**
Far right: A waxy texture is characteristic of many orchid flowers. **(SY)**

Left/Bottom left: Orchids like **Liparis foetulenta** and **Eria** are epiphytes, growing in some convenient nook or crevice well above the ground. (SY) (TYP)
Bottom right: **Bulbophyllum patens.** (KR)
Below: **Spathoglottis plicata.** (TS)

Above: Within a single hectare of forest there may be over 100 sorts of trees. **(MG)**

Facing page
A great variety of lichens and other tiny plants can be found growing on leaves and tree trunks. Different species grow upon different textured surfaces, some in light and some in shady conditions. For water they must depend on mists and whatever flows down the trunk during rain.

The Forest Shade

Descending the tree tower, below the crowns of the emergent trees and the main tree layer, we immediately enter the gloom of the forest shade, where about half the sunlight is shut out. Weather instruments set at different levels on the tower showed interesting inversions of the air layers, a layer of warm air trapped below the cooler canopy in the early morning.

The straight unbranched trunks stand like massive pillars, presenting what appears to be a very bleak place to live. But in the tropical rain forest all spaces are used by some plant or animal, and this all adds up to give the forest its tremendous diversity.

A second look at the bare trunks shows they are mottled and blotched by small plants. These are lichens, the co-operative effort of algae and fungi living together to make up a single organism. Frequently they are greyish or greenish and several species of moths and spiders mimic these colours to make themselves almost invisible.

Patient waiting will reveal the sudden movement of an animal in the

(KSN)

(SLG)

(JD)

(A/ME)

Top: The slender squirrel **Sunda-
sciurus tenuis** has a very varied diet
including seeds, fruits, tree bark and
resin, and even some insects. (MS)
Middle: A leaf-like disguise is
common to many forest crickets and
katydids. (PG)
Bottom: The ferocious appearance
of **Gonocephalus borneensis** is
misleading: this lizard will remain
absolutely still to avoid being seen,
or run away rather than bite. (KBH)

gloom. Squirrels and lizards of many kinds can be found here, and perhaps the occasional flying lemur *Cynocep halus variegatus*, such as the one that frequented the tree tower itself for a few days. Arboreal skinks scour the bare tree trunks for flies and spiders. Flying lizards signal to one another with their brightly coloured throat flaps and, if that does not work, they glide dramatically from tree to tree. The giant gecko, *Gecko stentor,* can be heard calling by day but only at night does it emerge from its dark crevice under the bark.

Ten metres down the tower, the vegetation is a straggling layer of young trees, palms, and below them shrubs. This layer effectively cuts off much of the remaining light, so that only one to three per cent of full sunlight filters down to the forest floor.

While the shrubs and palms are adapted to living in the deep shade, young saplings of the giant forest trees grow slowly until, with luck, a canopy tree dies and so creates a gap with sufficient light and space for a youngster to take its place.

Left: Leafhoppers resemble cicadas both in shape and in their diet of plant sap. (**A/ME**)
Below: Moths are adept at picking the background best able to conceal them. (**JD**)

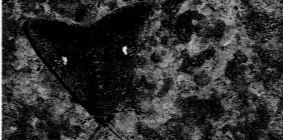

A very different group of birds lives in this lower layer from those that forage within the canopy. Babblers of many kinds frequent the forest undergrowth, though one may be common on hill slopes and another over level ground, one ranging widely and another restricted to a very narrow zone. Smaller woodpeckers live here, like the ridiculously tiny Rufous piculet, *Sasia abnormis*, about the size of a man's thumb. A bulbul may be glimpsed briefly as it darts between the trees, while trogons sit quietly and may easily escape notice despite their brilliant colours. Almost 200 species of birds were recorded in Endau-Rompin during the expedition, the vast majority confined to the forest, and many of them characteristic of this lower level vegetation.

Above: In the middle layer, trees begin their life by growing rapidly upwards, forming tall slender pole-like trunks, their stems only thickening once their crowns have reached the light. (LYK)
Top right: Blue-winged leafbird **Chloropsis cochinchinensis.** (MS)
Below right: Brown Fulvetta **Alcippe brunneicauda.** (MS)

Top: Several similar-looking bulbuls, including the Cream-vented bulbul **Pycnonotus simplex,** frequent the logging tracks at Endau-Rompin. (MS)
Bottom: Another common bird of the forest edge, the Orange-bellied flowerpecker **Dicaeum trigono-stigma,** is also found at Padang Temambong. (MS)

Several kinds of frogs in the forest, including the forest bush frog **Polypedates macrotis** *(left) and the spotted froglet* **Nyctixalus pictus** *(right), are adapted to climbing. Their adaptations include broad sticky webs and sucker-like tips to their toes.* **(KR) (PG)**

Tree-frogs are found in this lower layer. These are a varied group with 30 species in Peninsular Malaysia, all of them with expanded disc-like toe and finger tips, sticky with mucus, that help them cling to leaves and twigs. Wallace's flying frog, *Rhacophorus nigropalmatus,* one of the larger tree frogs with especially big feet, is able to parachute by spreading its webbed toes to break its fall. It was one of several species present at Endau-Rompin. They are, however, very difficult to spot except at night with the aid of a torchlight which reflects their eyes in the darkness. The expedition herpetologist once disturbed a paradise tree snake, *Chrysopelea paradisi,* which slithered rapidly up a tree. A few moments later he was surprised by a large tree toad which shot out of the crown of the same tree; no doubt it had met the snake!

A leaf by leaf search reveals a wealth of insect life among the shrubs. There are caterpillars of all shapes and sizes, silently and steadily chomping on the leaves and flowers. Stick insects may suddenly be flushed from hiding while praying mantids lie in wait for unwary small insects. An enormous yellow leaf insect, known as *Heteropteryx dilatata,* was found in the undergrowth right next to the expedition base camp, remarkable for its colour as this species is usually bright green.

It is perhaps surprising at first to find that the inside of the forest is so empty and much of the ground is bare of vegetation. If we dig into the ground we find the reason — the ground is full of the roots of trees, lianes, shrubs and palms, so small herbs have a stiff fight to find a foothold.

Although herbs are few and far between they are easily spotted, especially as they usually have very pretty flowers. Good examples are the gin-

The defences of caterpillars include startling false eyes on a hawk-moth caterpillar (top) and fiercely stinging hairs on a limacodid caterpillar (bottom). **(JD) (KBH)**

Above: The front legs of the praying mantis bear sharp spines which grasp the prey firmly and control its struggles while the mantis is feeding. **(PG)**

Top left/Left: When they are moving stick insects are easy to spot; many species have brightly coloured wings which attract attention when they fly. As soon as they settle they become very inconspicuous. **(PG) (SY)**

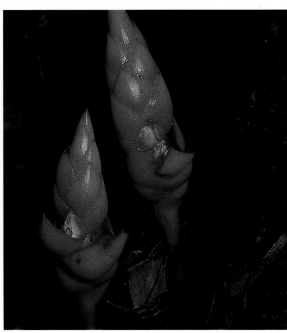

gers — often blessed with flamboyantly red flowers — and wild relatives of the delicate African violet family. Some of these herbs are very rare and are only found on Gunung Janing, such as *Phyllagathis cordata,* or only in Johor, such as *Didymocarpus densifolius.*

Endau-Rompin has proved to have several plants with such restricted distributions, termed "endemic" to the particular region they inhabit. Most of them are confined to the sandstone tops of ridges. This is logical: the hills are quite isolated from other hill ranges in the Peninsula, and this may have allowed the gradual development of special characteristics in some plants, making them increasingly distinct from their near relatives.

Top left: Wild ginger **Alpinia mutica** (KBH)
Top right: Most gingers have red, orange or yellow flowers. **Boesenbergia** *is unusual with its delicate clusters of white blossom, which emerge near the base of the leaves.* (KBH)
Right: Wild ginger **Zingiber griffithii** (KBH)

Facing page: **Didymocarpus densifolius,** *growing on rocks in swift, torrential streams, is known only from Johor and from Pulau Tioman. It flowers gregariously, all plants in a cluster blossoming together.* (KR)

Above: Amidst mosses on the forest floor grows a slender leguminous creeper in the bean family. (JD)
Right: Giant millipedes Julus sp. forage for lichens and moss. (PG)
Far right: The under-storey of the forest is not difficult to walk through. The ground is covered with leaf litter, and most of the smaller plants are palms, gingers and seedlings of the forest trees. (KSN)

On The Forest Floor

Plants with attractive flowers can be in the minority on the forest floor. Besides the seedlings of trees there are ferns, selaginellas, mosses and other more obscure groups. The blue-leafed Peacock selaginella, *Selaginella wildenowii*, immediately attracts attention. Around the bases of tree trunks or on thin tree stems are clusters of mosses. The Endau area proved to be very rich in mosses, with more species than are recorded from the lowlands of Taman Negara (Peninsular Malaysia's only national park), and some which were not previously known from Peninsular Malaysia.

In some areas, tree seedlings are so common that they form a green carpet. This is where a big tree has fruited a year or two before. But the patch of new growth is short-lived. Unless they are lucky enough to germinate in a spot that gets enough

Above: Peacock-plant **Selaginella wildenowii** (KSN)
Below: **Selaginella intermedia** *forms carpets in shady forest. The selaginellas are placed within their own group, separate from ferns or mosses.* (JD)

light, the seedlings will persist only a few years in the deep shade. Even if a big tree happens to die, allowing light in, only one or two of the seedlings will succeed in the stiff competition to reach the light.

Many animals large and small are confined to the ground. From rats, mouse-deer *Tragulus* spp., barking deer *Muntiacus muntjak*, sambar deer *Cervus unicolor*, bearded pig *Sus barbatus*, tapir *Tapirus indicus*, rhinoceros and elephant that quietly go about their own business feeding on leaves and fruits, to the feared tiger – they are all found in abundance at Endau. More than 60 different kinds of mammals were recorded during the expedition. It was common to see fresh prints of tapir and tiger *Panthera tigris*, close to camp. Once the remains of a partly eaten pig were discovered, indicating that a tiger was in the area. On another occasion a line of tiger footprints, freshly made the previous night, was followed for more than two kilometres along a trail. A tiger even came sniffing around base camp one quiet night when only two people were sleeping there. Tigers can travel enormous distances in a single night, usually alone, though a mother will be accompanied by her cubs until they are several months old. The abundance of prey at Endau-Rompin, especially wild pigs and bearded pigs, as well as the lack of disturbance, no doubt contributed to the frequency with which the tracks of tigers were seen there.

Bearded pigs are a Johor specialty. Named because of the very bristly snout of the adult male, they were only discovered in Peninsular Malaysia during the 20th century, and have been recorded in all the southern states. Fossils have been reported from as far north as Kelantan, but in historical times their range has contracted, perhaps in response to competition from a second species, the

common wild pig, as well as hunting by man. In Borneo, where only the bearded pig is found, huge herds migrate through the forest at certain seasons, seeking fallen fruits. Similar migrations once took place in Peninsular Malaysia, and pig-sticking as herds crossed the Sungai Endau was in former days a huge source of meat for villagers such as the Kampung Peta Orang Hulu.

Definite tracks of the Sumatran rhinoceros, three-toed and more than 17 centimetres broad, were seen on more than one occasion. The tracks are sometimes hard to tell from those of tapir but the rhinoceros has a larger foot, and the toes are much more rounded. Endau-Rompin has long been known as a stronghold of the rhinoceros in Peninsular Malaysia, with the highest concentration somewhat to the west of the main expedition area. Population estimates for the whole country have varied widely, from 25 to more than 100 individuals, of which a large percentage live in the Endau watershed.

Most of the animals seen on the ground are of humbler kinds, like the

Facing page: The study of wild bananas **Musa gracilis** *was interrupted when the plants were trampled by elephants* **Elephas maximus.** *(*TMNY)*
Above: Active at night, but also sometimes by day, the lesser mouse-deer **Tragulus javanicus** *feeds on fallen fruits and other plant material. Twice, mouse-deer were seen swimming across the Sungai Jasin. (*AJ)*
Centre: Animals like tigers **Panthera tigris** *can only survive in large protected areas. (*TMNY)*
Below: Bearded pig **Sus barbatus.** *(*MK)*

horned toad, master of camouflage, whose kwang-kwang call foretells imminent rain. Despite its bright colours, the little jewel frog *Rana signata*, is even harder to spot, and it is sometimes necessary to scan the river banks where it lives inch by inch to locate it.

The bare ground of the forest floor is covered by leaf litter but it is by no means dead. It provides sustenance for thousands of mushrooms, toadstools and lesser fungi which decompose the fallen leaves and twigs and release back into the system the nutrients that the green plants need to live. Some of the more cryptic fungi can best be seen by night, when they glow faintly in the leaf litter, giving the impression of dappled moonlight even when there is no moon.

Not all decomposers are fungi: some like *Thismia*, produce flowers. One species, *Thismia arachnites*, is so rare that the plant at Endau is only the third ever found in Peninsular Malaysia.

Above: Noisy but hard to spot, the Jewel Frog **Rana signata.** (KBH)
Right: **Varanus rudicollis** *is a monitor lizard restricted to forest.* (MS)
Facing page: Malaysian Horned Toad **Megophrys monticola** (PG)

(KR)

(A/ME)

Above: **Thismia aseroe,** *a flowering plant without chlorophyll, obtains nutrients from the rotting vegetation on which it grows.* (KR)

Scientists found a huge variety of fungi in the expedition area. The fruiting bodies, in the form of mushrooms or toadstools, represent only a small proportion of the living fungus; a much greater bulk of tissue may lie within the soil, as fine thread-like hyphae.

(KR)

(JD)

(FSPN)

(A/ME)

(A/ME)

(A/ME)

(KR)

Above: The long-legged termite
Longipeditermes longipes *eats leaf litter.* (LC)

Top right: Great quantities of cellulose from dead wood are returned to the nutrient cycle of the forest by the action of termites. (KSN)
Bottom right: **Hospitalitermes,** *a termite nesting in stumps and feeding on lichens.* (RBS)

Termites are particularly important in the leaf litter as they play a major role in the breakdown of dead wood. Many kinds of termites occur in the forest and they can often be told apart by their choice of nest site: a hillock of soil on the ground, or inside a tree, or attached to the side of a tree trunk, or perhaps even underground. Just like the leaf-eating monkeys, the termites themselves are unable to digest cellulose and rely upon a selection of bacteria, known as the microflora, living within their guts. The termites break down the decaying wood physically with their sharp jaws, the bacteria break it down chemically, so each benefits from the assistance of the other.

The Hill Slopes

The tree tower at Endau-Rompin was sited near the foot of Gunung Janing Barat, where the trees included keruing, rengas and meranti. Rengas, when the bark is cut, exudes a black sap which causes blisters and rashes on the skin. One expedition member had to be flown out by helicopter, so severe was his skin reaction. Rengas was one of the commoner trees both on the hill slopes and on the plateau.

Walking uphill from the tower, changes appear in the surrounding vegetation. The lush growth of ginger, palas *Licuala* and pinang *Pinanga* palms is gradually reduced, and plants such as tongkat ali *Eurycoma longifolia* and the walking stick palm *Rhopaloblaste singaporensis*, become commoner. Then, quite suddenly, fan palms appear.

On the upper slopes, it is the fan palm which predominates. This palm, a kind of serdang palm, proved to be a new species. The large tough leaves of these palms, resistant to decay, blanket the ground on falling, smothering the seedlings of other forest trees. Because they are tough,

these leaves are not palatable to insects nor do the palm's fruits seem to be eaten by animals. In consequence the fan palm forest seems relatively lifeless. But aesthetically this forest is very pleasing, with its large fringed leaves forming regular silhouettes against the sky.

In the fan palm forest is a rock face caused by the weathering of sandstone. It is on these rocks that *Phyllagathis cordata*, a herb endemic to Gunung Janing, and a new species of *Didymocarpus, D. falcata*, can be found.

On the ridge of Gunung Janing Barat at 450 metres is a water-logged area where hill swamp forest grows. This is a type of heath forest, much better known in Sarawak than in Peninsular Malaysia. It differs markedly from other forest types because its canopy is low and more open, the trees are much smaller and pole-like, and the ground is water-logged and covered by sedges. Epiphytes are more abundant here, partly because of the damper conditions, and so are ant plants and insectivorous plants.

This swampy forest covers only a small area, too small to support any special community of animals. Most of the wildlife seen there are visitors from the taller forest beyond. The occasional group of pigs wanders through; a tapir pauses for a few minutes, chewing off the nutritious bark of a small tree; a troop of banded leaf monkeys *Presbytis melalophos* calls briefly, before descending the hill again.

A more extensive and much more extreme version of heath forest was discovered on Padang Temambong (700 metres), which is topped by a gently sloping sandstone plateau, with a raised rim. In places the sandstone has weathered down to a fine white sand. The boggier areas are covered by a large sedge with strap-shaped leaves, *Machaerina maingayi*,

*Above: The cut bark of **Gluta elegans** exudes a highly irritant sap which causes severe skin rashes.* **(KR)**

*Above: Above the sandstone cliff of
Gunung Janing Barat, fan palms
become abundant.* (KSN)
*Left: Fan palm **Livistona endauensis**,
endemic to the expedition area.* (PG)

Right: Two climbing species of **Dischidia** *intertwine.* **(KSN)**

Below: Waterlogging in the swampy heath forest strongly affects the plant community. **(KSN)**

and by pitcher plants. On better drained soil, groups of straggly trees are surrounded by shrubs and ferns, several of which are characteristic of much higher montane vegetation. Examples are the ferns *Matonia pectinata* and *Gleichenia microphylla*, the orchid *Spathoglottis aurea*, and the *Machaerina* sedge itself.

The *Machaerina* bog is drained by trickles of water, which from the air look like animal trails. In fact once formed by water these bare sandy channels are used as travel routes by various animals. Wild pigs *Sus scrofa* use them a lot, and may themselves be a factor in maintaining the short grassy vegetation. They dig up roots

Left: **Nepenthes ampullaria** *never grows more than a few inches above the ground.* **(GC)**
Below left: Ground pitchers of **Nepenthes rafflesiana** *are much stouter than the aerial ones.* **(GC)**
Below: The slender pitcher plant **Nepenthes gracilis.** **(KSN)**

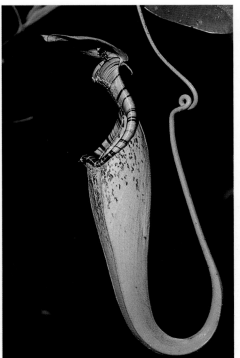

by probing with their mobile snouts, and they can roll up whole sections of the grassy turf like a carpet.

The trickles of water drain into larger streams which have scoured away the soil down to the pink bedrock of sandstone. Along the streams grow gnarled *Leptospermum* trees, so stunted they look like bonsai trees. At the edge of the plateau the water drains over cascades down into the surrounding tall forest.

The contrast in the stature of the forest and the number of species between the impoverished plateau and the surrounding tall forest is also reflected in the paucity of animal life. The plateau is almost silent: few cicadas whine, the dawn chorus is muted. During the day few animals are seen — a rat, a squirrel, three kinds of frogs, and only a few birds and butterflies. At night there may be more visitors, including pigs and the leopard whose tracks were found in the damp soil. An interesting feature of the plateau is that despite its isolation, a little open patch within a sea of tall forest, a few open-country animals have managed to reach it. The dark-necked tailorbird *Orthotomus atrogularis* is one of these, and the oriental scops owl *Otus sunia* is another. Even the common village-living tree frog, katak pisang, *Polypedates leucomystax* has somehow arrived.

The silence of the plateau is eerie, and gives credence to the Orang Hulu tales that it is a holy place where spirits live. In the oppressive silence one can almost imagine the presence of the spirits.

*Above: Open **padang** vegetation is maintained by a combination of soil type and depth, poor drainage and mammal activity.* **(SLG)**
Right: Padang Temambong, characterised by ferns, sedges and pandans. **(DW)**

Top: Gnarled **Leptospermum flavescens.** (TJH)
Left: Water trickles amongst the stunted vegetation. (SLG)

medicinal plants

The people of Kampung Peta, though settled in a permanent village, have a high regard for the surrounding forest. Whenever collecting medicinal plants they replant a section "so that something is put back". Many of the medicines prepared are used to treat problems in pregnancy and childbirth. (A/ME)

Tropical forests are extremely rich in plant species, containing more than half the world's flora. Very few of these plants have been studied adequately for their medicinal properties but those that have been studied have contributed greatly to the pharmacological weapons that modern man needs to fight disease and illness.

Already, 25 per cent of the world's pharmaceutical products come from tropical forests, with an estimated annual retail value of US$20 billion. Well known examples of these are quinine, which comes from the bark of the cinchona tree, and is used to treat malaria; the cancer chemotherapy drugs, from the Madagascar periwinkle, *Catharanthus rosea*, hypertension drugs from the Indian snakeroot plant, *Rauwolfia* spp. and oral contraceptives obtained from Mexican plants of the genus *Dioscorea*.

The Orang Hulu from Kampung Peta have developed a close relationship with the forest since forest products have traditionally formed the basis of their livelihood. As a result they have built up a large "drugstore" of plants which have healing values. While they do use easily available commercial pharmaceutical products, the relatively isolated communities still rely on plant medicines for certain ailments. Consequently, the Orang Hulu are very aware of the need to conserve such plants in the forest. This is reflected in their practice of replanting a portion of each plant they collect.

During the Endau-Rompin expedition some of the community elders were asked if they could identify some of the plants they used for these purposes. This resulted in a list of more than 50 species, with information on the uses and methods of preparing each.

The uses varied from alleviation of pains associated with bruises, bee stings, snakebite, toothache, stomach-ache, rashes, itches and kidney pains, to healing haemorrhoids, tongue and mouth ulcers, bone fractures and malaria. The fern *Schizaea wagneri* looking like dried twigs 8-20 centimetres long, was used as an aphrodisiac. Stomach troubles were treated by mixing two spices with a fruticose lichen. There were also medicines for diabetes, diarrhoea, rheumatism, coughs, anaemia, dropsy and smallpox.

A large proportion of the plants were used in preventive medicine and health tonics, as well as aphrodisiacs and for matters relating to contraception, pregnancy, childbirth and postnatal complications.

Most of these plants are not in regular use outside the forest and rural areas, but the fame of some has spread. The best known of these is the tongkat ali, *Eurycoma longifolia*. Although the Orang Hulu are well

Anisophyllea disticha. (CT)

Wild yam **Dioscorea** sp., used in various medications. (SLG)

Twisted pods of **Archidendron** sp. (A/ME)

Dipteris lobbiana. (KSN)

Lumbah **Curculigo latifolia.** (JD)

Roots, such as those of **Pentaphragma flocculosa,** are the most commonly used plant parts for medicine. (KR)

Forrestia griffithii. (SY)

The roots of **Rennellia elongata** are said by residents of Kampung Peta to prevent bleeding after childbirth. (WKM)

Roots of **Ancistrocladus** may help with abdominal pains, after mixing with seven herbs. (WKM)

Black lily, *Tacca integrifolia.* (SY)

Tongkat Ali *Eurycoma longifolia.* (SY)

Schizaea wagneri. (HM)

Fruticose lichens *Usnea* sp. are mixed with spices as a cure for stomach troubles. (SLG)

aware of its reputed aphrodisiacal properties, they also use the root for toothache and kidney pains. Another famous aphrodisiac is the small shrub dedawai *Smilax calophylla* which, when combined with the fern, payong ali, *Dipteris lobbiana,* and the rattan, rotan batu *Calamus insignis* provides a health tonic.

Some plants are used as medicines both by the Orang Hulu and by rural people elsewhere, but not necessarily for the same purpose. Tubers of the black lily or keladi murai, *Tacca integrifolia,* are used by Malay villagers as a treatment for rashes. At Kampung Peta, its leaves are considered the important part, to be applied as a hot poultice for rheumatism and aching limbs. Malays use the roots of *Forrestia griffithii* to treat fevers, but the Orang Hulu use them for snake and centipede bites.

The fruits of lumbah, *Curculigo latifolia* are often used as a sweetener and to increase appetite after fevers. The fruit itself does not taste sweet but has the curious property of making anything taken soon after it taste sweet. The plant is also used to treat fevers, smallpox, tumours, and kidney stones.

The large climbing fern ribu-ribu, *Lygodium circinnatum* is used for kidney pains. The fruit of pinang puteri, *Pinanga limosa,* is mixed with *Smilax* and taken as a contraceptive and abortifacient.

Within the Endau-Rompin forest alone there are plants which may provide important medicines in the future. Recently, a plant from the forests of the Amazon was used in the effort to develop a vaccine against Acquired Immune Deficiency Syndrome (AIDS). Clearly, without tropical forests, the world would lose a valuable source of possible new medicines.

along the
RIVER
COURSES

along the river courses

Endau-Rompin has wonderfully scenic rivers. Some stretches, around and below the base camp, have been influenced by man's activities. A much greater portion remain uninhabited and nature has taken its own course in shaping the landscape.

River systems are usually defined in terms of their catchment areas, the areas from which they gather their water. At Endau-Rompin there are three. The Sungai Endau catchment drains an area of about 420 square kilometres, and the smaller Sungai Selai about 170 square kilometres. These two basins are sharply defined by the steep hills which act as watersheds between them, while a third basin feeds the Sungai Rompin on the Pahang side of the border.

A distinctive plant community lines the river banks. Smaller plants like the fern *Dipteris lobbiana* are well adapted to withstand the rush of floods, their strap-like leaves offering little resistance to the flow of water. Amongst the larger trees of the river banks the pelawan, *Tristania whiteana* is easy to recognise: a relative of the Australian gum trees, its bark splits and peels off.

Left: Rivers and roads: highways through the forest. **(SLG)**
Below: A tiny trickle may be the first source of a big river. **(RA)**

Previous page
Main: Buaya Sangkut, an aerial view from the north. (HHH)
Inset, top: *Eriocaulon sexangulare* on the bank of Sungai Jasin. (SLG)
Inset, bottom: Black-spotted sticky frog **Kalophrynus pleurostigma.** (PG)

Left: Sungai Sempanong. (KSN)

*Above: Pelawan **Tristania
whiteana,** the most easily identified
riverside tree.* (KR)

*Left: Different plants prefer slow
and fast water.* (KSN) (JD)

Plants In The River

Botanists and zoologists working at Endau-Rompin found that the excellent water quality of these rivers was reflected in the kinds of aquatic plants and animals living there. Two genera of red algae, *Batrachospermum* and *Compsopogon*, were very abundant in the fast-flowing tributaries, thriving in the very pure water. These algae formed thick, dark red tufts which clung tenaciously to the rocks. After the monsoon, many species had their populations reduced or redistributed by the raging waters, but the persistent short-tufted *Compsopogon* was still abundant. *Batrachospermum*, with its mucilaginous filaments, looked like beaded strands of frogs' eggs in the water, hence its common name "frogspawn". A new species of *Batrachospermum* was discovered at Sungai Zain. Another red alga genus, *Ballia*, is known to include species which have migrated from the sea. One species was found as far inland as Sungai Sempanong.

Thick streaming masses of light and dark green filaments covered the rocks in the shallow, slow-flowing and sunlit tributaries. These slimy masses, dominated by *Spirogyra*, and *Zygnema*, and *Trentepohlia*, covered in places entire surfaces of rock. They were the most easily recognized of the algae. All three are called "green algae", but while *Spirogyra* with its helical chloroplasts and *Zygnema* with its star-shaped ones really are green, *Trentepohlia* coloured the rocks with varied hues of orange due to the carotenoid pigment in its cells.

In quiet shaded pools, blue-green filaments of *Scytonema* and *Lyngbya* were attached to the roots of trees and shrubs lining the water's edge. Here a host of organisms, ranging from microscopic animals to baby prawns and fish, found both a sanctuary and a feeding ground. Inconspicuous though they may be, algae are the silent oxygenators of the water, producing oxygen by photosynthesis and simultaneously removing the dissolved nutrients washed into the rivers. They form the basis of many food chains which often end with fish and finally man.

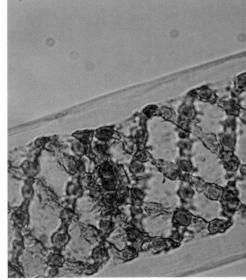

*Above: Algae like **Spirogyra** and **Zygnema** tangle together in a thick green soup. (PSM)*
Right: Even fast-flowering water contains algae. (PSM)
*Far right: The green alga **Spirogyra**, easily identified by its spiral chloroplasts. (PSM)*

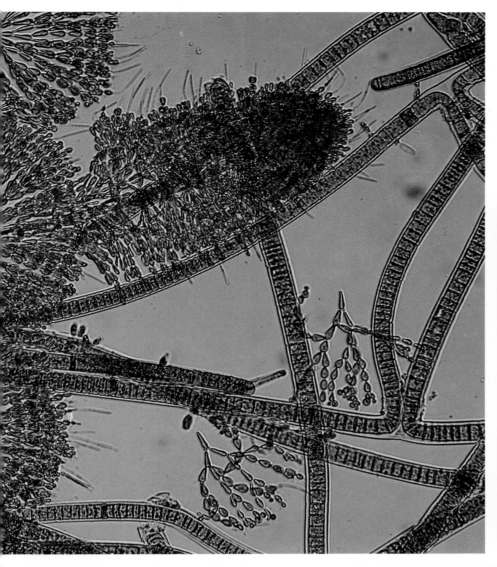

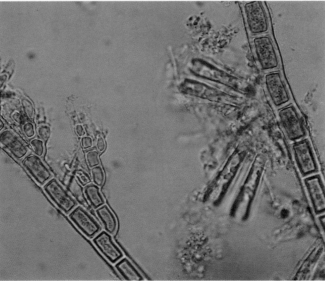

Left: Whorl of **Batrachospermum** *mingle with the bootlace* **Scyto-nema.** *(PSM)*

Above: A densely branching **Batrachospermum,** *like a slimy string of frogs' spawn when out of water. (PSM)*
Left: Red alga **Ballia** *sp.. (PSM)*

Top: The sandy bed of Sungai Anak Jasin, a good spot for fish. (KSN)
Above: The cautious prawn, ever ready to hide beneath a rock or leaf. (JD)

Top right: Bujok *Channa lucius* (*TMNY)
Bottom right: Many freshwater fishes like toman *Channa micropeltes* are dappled grey. (*KSN)

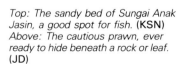

Frogs And Fishes

At least 43 different kinds of fish were found in the rivers around base camp. This was just a sample from a small part of the river system, and undoubtedly many more species exist in the habitats yet to be surveyed. Commonest of all was the lampam, *Barbus schwanenfeldi.* The average size of these fish was considerably larger at Endau than at other rivers in Peninsular Malaysia, indicating that fishing pressure is still relatively low here. One fish, now quite rare elsewhere in the country, but found in several of the smaller rivers, was the harlequin, *Rasbora heteromorpha,* a popular aquarium fish.

Kelah, *Tor douronensis* is regarded as one of the best eating fish, and has great potential for aquaculture. It was one of the fish popular with residents of Kampung Peta, but a commoner and much more easily caught fish was the common catfish *Mystus planiceps,* known locally as Baung Akar. This required careful handling though, because it has a long sharp spine on its back. Sebarau, *Hampala macrolepidota* and toman, *Channa micropeltes* were other common fish.

Several rare fishes were found in Endau-Rompin. As for other aquatic animals, their diversity was linked to the many different habitats available. At Kuala Marong was a sluggish pool, dark and deep. At Buaya Sangkut very shallow reaches alternated with tumbling rapids. Some of the smaller rivers had smooth sandy beds, while others were very rocky. Each had its own characteristic fish, prawns and frogs.

One of the prettiest tadpoles lived at Buaya Sangkut, just above the waterfall where water an inch or two deep lapped over flat sheets of rock. Each tadpole was as transparent as glass, but for a black saddle, a red patch on its head, and a single iridescent golden spot on its forehead.

Above: Flowing down from Padang Temambong, the Sungai Lemakoh. **(RA)**
Right/Far right: The clear-water pools of Sungai Marong form a cool and rocky home. **(MK)**
Above right: Pools along Sungai Zain contained many freshwater prawns. **(KR)**

quoise speckles on its legs, was found inside hollow logs at the water's edge, where it evidently intended to cause maximum difficulty for scientists to find it. Even far away from rivers on the top of Gunung Janing Barat were little frogs, their tadpoles living inside the cups of pitcher plants.

Some birds, too, were often to be seen along the rivers. A Lesser Fishing-eagle, *Ichthyophaga humilis* often perched in a riverside tree. As a boat crossed the river the same bird would be disturbed again and again, flying a few hundred yards before settling, only to be disturbed as the boat approached once more.

JOURNEYS

The rivers provided a focus for many expedition scientists. Some were directly concerned with the rivers and their inhabitants. A year-long survey monitored changes in the water levels, in an attempt to calculate the volume of water discharged. Fish, frogs and a population of green prawns not far from base camp were the subjects of special studies. Geologists found the exposed rocks along the river banks a major source of information, and travelling by river enabled them to piece together the geological puzzle over a wide area.

Cross-country hikers made waterfalls their targets. Small camps were built at Jeram Upeh Guling and at Buaya Sangkut, two of the main waterfalls along the Sungai Jasin, and served as bases for work some distance from headquarters. More enterprising travellers tried to end each day's hike at a stream or river. Sometimes they succeeded and sometimes they did not, as the following stories tell.

Some of these tadpoles, a species of tree-frog, were taken back to the laboratory to await their metamorphosis into little frogs. They proved remarkably adept at escaping, always at night, and the species was never identified.

Frogs live in the most surprising places. At least four species live up in trees, including Wallace's Flying Frog, *Rhacophorus nigropalmatus* and a new species of tree-frog named after expedition patron and Malaysia's first Prime Minister, Tunku Abdul Rahman. The pretty Blue-legged Tree-frog *Rhacophorus bimaculatus*, with tur-

The journey to Gunung Beremban began by helicopter. **(LFS)**

Giant frogs **Rana blythi** *were found at Kuala Kemapan* **(SLG)**

Kuala Kemapan, starting point for botanical and geological surveys. **(SLG)**

Gunung Beremban

A survey of the Gunung Beremban area was carried out in September 1985 by a team of 12 scientists and their assistants, comprising foresters, geologists, botanists, expedition leader Dr Kiew Bong Heang and his botanist wife Ruth, who writes:

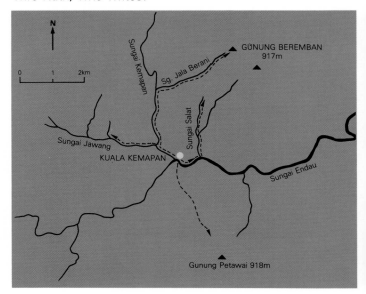

Where should the headquarters of the proposed Endau-Rompin Park be sited? One suggestion was the foot of Gunung Beremban. That was why we visited the area. Also, our geologists were keen to examine the geology of the Gunung Beremban summit.

An RMAF helicopter made our survey possible in five days. It dropped us on a boulder island in Sungai Endau just below Kuala Kemapan. We felt quite alone and abandoned when the helicopter disappeared. A sub-camp was built high on the bank above the confluence and by the time it was dark we were comfortably installed under a tarpaulin roof.

The Sungai Endau at this point is about the size of Sungai Jasin at base camp and is joined by a slightly smaller river, the Sungai Kemapan. At the confluence is a beautiful, deep pool ideal for swimming.

On the first day (Tuesday), the party split with Kiew and I joining geologists Danny Walker and Idris Mohamad in conquering Gunung Beremban by following Sungai Salat to its source. We set off down Sungai Endau and turned up Sungai Salat which was slow-flowing because its mouth was clogged with sand and the small riverine pandan. At first the Salat meandered, and gradually the sandy bottom became more muddy and was bordered by swamp. It was not long before the gradient became steeper and the stream bed rocky. We slipped and scrambled along. Some cascades were sloping, others were sheer four to seven-metre precipices.

Kiew and I cautiously skirted the waterfalls, often on our hands and knees, while the intrepid geologists climbed straight up the slippery rock faces looking for any geological features that the river had exposed.

Eventually the Sungai Salat petered out into a narrow boulder-strewn watercourse that cut into the steep slope — but we were not at the top. It was then that Idris cheerfully remarked that we had probably followed one of the many tributaries and anyway geologists frequently lose their way! Actually it was easy to get lost as many of the smaller streams were not marked on the map, having been drawn from aerial photos.

On Wednesday, Idris and Danny set off with camping gear, determined to make it to the summit by going up the Sungai Kemapan followed by the Sungai Jala Berani. Would they find sandstone on the top? This was the first time that geologists ascended the summit (917 metres) and surveyed the geology of the mountain.

The rest of us stayed on the steep, lower slopes of Gunung Beremban. We followed a steep ridge where we encountered argus pheasant display areas, one of which was old and another apparently still in use. The botanists, led by K.M. Wong and L.G. Saw, persisted up the steep slope to find *Livistona* palm forest where a massive club-moss grew epiphytically in the crown of a palm.

Thursday saw the botanists setting off for Gunung Pertawai, while Kiew and I waded and sometimes swam up the Sungai Endau, to record the changing features of the river and its riverine flora. Above the confluence with Sungai Kemapan, the Sungai Endau narrowed. Instead of wide, shallow stretches with a bed of small boulders, there were deep straight stretches alternating with cascades, some arranged in series. So we were forced to abandon the stream and cut a path through the forest. In places on the banks, tree trunks and debris left by floods showed that the flood level was at least 1.6 metres above the usual water level. Above the Sungai Kemapan, the Sungai Endau is narrower than the Sungai Jasin at base camp but still carried a considerable amount of water. We decided it was quicker to return through the forest and found a well-marked Orang Hulu trail on the south bank.

That night Kiew led a team in a search for frogs along the Endau and Salat.

The next day, Kiew and I followed a small stream, the Sungai Jawang (a tributary of the Sungai Kemapan) upstream. This proved to be interesting as its lower stretches were moderately slow flowing with sandy banks or swampy muddy areas, and apparently not subject to flooding. Here several plants such as *Nitella* (a macroscopic green alga), eel grass, the aquarium plant *Cryptocoryne affinis,* and a small herb *Torenia peduncularis* grew, an assemblage of plants not yet encountered in the other torrential rivers in the Endau area. Eventually the Sungai Jawang narrowed into a gorge with cascades (which we were forced to skirt) above which was a very pretty waterfall, about 7 metres high. From then on the stream had a flat rocky bed interrupted by cascades. These rocky banks were fringed with the fern *Dipteris lobbiana.* This upper stretch is very similar to that of Sungai Marong.

That night Idris and Danny returned. They had made it to the top, although it had taken them more than a day. They found that the mountain is ignimbrite until right near the top where there is a narrow band of sandstone and that the vegetation on the top is not as nice and open as on Gunung Janing but is a veritable thicket of rattans, pandans and pole-like trees. Gunung Beremban is strangely shaped: it rises from the base with about a 45-degree slope but just below the summit the slope is much steeper (about 70 degrees) then the summit is almost flat.

The area was rich in wildlife: pigs were very common, we heard deer, probably sambar, dusky leaf monkeys, and gibbons, and saw pig-tailed macaques. In general, the area was both floristically and faunistically very similar to the base camp area.

Our survey showed that Kuala Jasin where the expedition had its base camp, would be more suitable as a base for the park. The foot of Gunung Beremban is less convenient because:

- There is no access by boat to Gunung Beremban as there are innumerable rapids between Kuala Jasin and Kuala Kemapan.

- Although the vegetation and wildlife is broadly similar, the Kuala Kemapan area is more rugged, making it tougher to see the same things. For example, from Kuala Jasin, the walk up Gunung Janing Barat is one to two hours. This takes one from the lowlands to the fan palm forest and finally up to the summit. However, the fan palm forest on Guning Beremban can only be reached in about four hours, and the summit, a whole day.

- It does not have such scenic features as the waterfall near Pulau Jasin (just an hour's walk from base camp) or the spectacular Buaya Sangkut waterfall (a six-hour walk), and

- It does not have the ecologically interesting Pulau Jasin, the swampy heath forest on Gunung Janing Barat (both within one to two hours' walk), nor the open "grassland" of Padang Temambong (six-hour walk).

Top: Easy to imagine how a crocodile might get stuck! **(PG)**
Above: Buaya Sangkut: one million gallons a minute. **(PG)**
Right: The many facets of Buaya Sangkut. **(SLG)**

Buaya Sangkut Waterfalls

Looking down Buaya Sangkut. (WYS)

A party of expedition members pioneered the route to Buaya Sangkut. Lee Su Win and Wong Khoon Meng describe what they found there:

There is an Orang Hulu legend which tells of an old crocodile that lived in the pools above a waterfall. One day, it went downriver and was trapped by the rocks, its body forming a fall. That was how the Buaya Sangkut waterfalls, the most spectacular "find" of the expedition, got their name, which means "trapped crocodile".

The 40 metre fall is located on the Sungai Jasin at about 300 metres above sea level. It was first spotted during a helicopter reconnaissance of the area by Malayan Nature Society members. Its location was checked on the map and a team of volunteers was sent to cut a trail to it.

The waterfall can be reached in six to ten hours' hike from the Kuala Jasin base camp — a distance of about 8 kilometres. Those who have visited the falls describe it as an awesome experience. The view from the edge of the forest was indeed spectacular — many tons of water plunging down a cliff-face 40 metres high and almost as wide.

The river tumbles down over three levels, and the lowest part of the falls is by far the greatest drop and the most majestic. An expedition sub-camp was sited at the second level of the falls. After thundering over the steep lowest part of the falls, the river continues through a narrow gorge which soon widens downstream and meanders past base camp on its way to the Sungai Endau.

The terrain on both sides of the Sungai Jasin at Buaya Sangkut is hilly, with ridges running down from slightly sloping plateaux. On these plateaux and ridges, a newly-discovered fan palm, *Livistona endauensis* and trees such as the hill pelawan, *Tristania merguiensis,* bintangor, *Calophyllum* spp. and the rengas tree *Gluta aptera* are common.

On the river banks, the vegetation mainly comprises trees like the river-side pelawan *Tristania whiteana,* the endemic simpoh puteh *Dillenia albiflos,* and huge keruing trees *Dipterocarpus costulatus* and *D. crinitus.* The walking-stick palm, *Rhopaloblaste singaporensis* with its clumps of erect stems and crowns of feathery fronds is also common in the river bank forests. Here and there on the river bank slopes, the rare clambering bamboo, *Racemobambos setifera* is encountered.

Nestling among other plants along the cool fringes of the stream are localised patches of Watson's Phyllanthus, *Phyllanthus watsoni* and the River Croton, *Croton rheophyticus,* both shrubs representative of the rubber tree

family, and known in the Malay Peninsula only from the Endau-Rompin area. Watson's Phyllanthus is not known outside the Endau basin, whereas the River Croton was recorded during the expedition for the first time in the Malay Peninsula, having been previously known to occur in West Borneo. A graceful tufted fern *Dipteris lobbiana,* with finely dissected fronds and only about half a metre tall, frequently decorates the river's edge next to calmer waters. It also sometimes occurs by the edge of torrential streams over boulders, on which can be found tiny thick-leafed rosettes of the fern *Grammitis universa,* the yellow orchid *Bulbophyllum vaginatum* and, occasionally, tufts of the pipewort *Eriocaulon sexangulare* nestled in the crevices.

As one leaves the water's edge and the Sungai Jasin pouring down in a thunderous roar, the forest seems distinctly quieter and only the occasional chorus of cicadas reminds us of other residents aside from the plants in this paradise. Along the river's edge and in rock pools, tiny translucent-bodied prawns dart in and out of crevices, seemingly unconcerned with the rest of nature's creation. And yet prawns, fishes and other creatures of the water, together with the plants and those magnificent falls, are together one system along the Sungai Jasin, the result of evolution and changes through the millenia.

The Plateau And The Falls

The normal route to the spectacular Buaya Sangkut water-fall from base camp is six to ten solid hours of trekking and climbing up the ridges of Bukit Segongong. Shaharin Yussof tells of a more "desirable" way to get there:

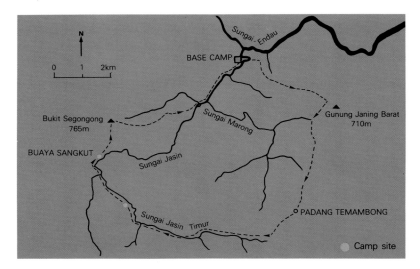

Umbrella palms *Johannesteysmannia altifrons* ornament the journey. (SY)

How does one savour the beauty and splendour of the Buaya Sangkut waterfall without the long and painful hours of trekking? Go via Padang Temambong, admittedly a longer route but far more interesting. The route is relatively easy but one must be prepared to spend two days and a night crossing the thick forest that separates Padang Temambong from the falls.

The walk across Padang Temambong is an adventure in itself. Crossing the open bog on the plateau we actually saw water seeping out of the boggy ground into the small trickles that eventually coalesced into streams and rivers such as the Sungai Marong, Sungai Lemakoh, and of course Sungai Jasin Timur. We passed several of these sedge-covered bogs to get to the southern edge of the plateau, at times fighting our way through thick, stunted forest interspersed with thickets of fern and pandan. The rim bore *Livistona* palm forest, and in contrast to the stifling still air of the central plateau, it was refreshingly breezy, with a clear view of the hills across the Lemakoh valley.

As we slipped and slid down the southern slope, more familiar forest appeared with many palms. The long-spined bayas *Oncosperma horridum* was noticeable, so was the walking stick palm, and of course the ubiquitous rattan and bertam, *Eugeissona tristis*. Pandans too were present, especially near the river.

On the level stretches, the sandy river bed itself supported a thick growth of river pandan, which slowed down the river so much that at times it was hard to see in which direction it flowed. The steeper rocky parts of the river were covered with the delicate fern *Dipteris lobbiana*.

Following the Sungai Lemakoh upstream was not easy. It meandered around interlocking ridges on either side. Sometimes the bends were swampy or made almost impassable by rattans and bertam. We also frequently encountered a giant pandan with large, broad and spiny leaves which, when rubbed against each other, sounded like galvanised sheet metal. This pandan too got in our way.

The river got smaller and smaller until it dried up and disappeared altogether. From there on, we had to rely on our compass. After about an hour of crossing ridges, we encountered more small streams but here they were flowing west. We followed one of these and it soon joined the larger Sungai Jasin Timur.

The trail we followed had lots of evidence of its makers and they included wild boar, tapir, elephants, and maybe even rhinoceros. Along the river banks we began to meet the umbrella palm, *Johannesteysmannia altifrons*, bamboos, and small fan palms, *Licuala* species. Rattans were in even greater abundance here.

The Sungai Jasin Timur meandered along a very level plain at an altitude of about 300 metres. This is an unusual plain since it is surrounded by higher hills. To the north is Padang Temambong and its ridge. To the south is an

*Spiny bertam palms **Eugeissona tristis,** the traveller's woe.* **(KSN)**

After two days, arriving at the falls. **(SY)**

unnamed range, to the south-west is Gunung Tiong, and west is Bukit Segongong, our goal.

At this point, it became imperative to find a site to camp for the night. We found one on higher ground near the river but off the game trail and pitched tent. At night the forest sounds changed and seemed much closer and more ominous. Everything outside the immediate vicinity of the campfire was in flickering shades of black and grey: nothing could be made out clearly. As morning approached, the frog and cricket noises gave way to cicadas and birds, while off in the distance, families of gibbons greeted the day. With the dawn everything turned to colour, and the surroundings seemed less claustrophobic.

Then we were off again through the forest along the river bank. As the day wore on, the river got wider and deeper. We made sure that we stayed on the southern side. Otherwise, it would be very difficult to cross the river when we reached the waterfall. At this point, the trail started to veer off from the river in order to reach a suitable ford across the tributaries. These were much larger and deeper at their mouths, and therefore harder to cross. As though by intuition, the trail makers had found a log that had conveniently fallen across the streams, making it easy to cross the sometimes muddy tributary.

During the night, we had heard the waterfall — a very faint, faraway sound, something like a well-travelled highway in the distance. As we got closer and closer, the

sound became more distinct, eventually becoming a loud hissing sound. Around this time, we reached a major confluence, where the Sungai Jasin Timur joined the Sungai Jasin. Again, the trail led to a very easy ford, allowing us to cross to the western side of the Sungai Jasin. At one point it looked as though the river pandan almost covered the whole river.

Now the river was twice as wide as before, sometimes almost 30 metres across and flowed so slowly that it didn't seem to move at all. Still, the rushing sound got louder. The river banks became steeper and steeper with the rocks, ground, and trees covered with moss. The trail petered out and we had to climb uphill, away from the river, to get to more level ground. Eventually we broke through to the trail again, which by now had been enlarged by scientists and other visitors who had reached Buaya Sangkut from the other direction — the "hard" way.

Following this trail, we reached the first of the Buaya Sangkut falls. Just below this fall was a nice pool for swimming. But we found it worthwhile to venture a little further downstream along the rocky river bank to the top of the main falls. Here was a sight to behold — a glorious view of the Sungai Jasin valley. Below, the water thrashed 40 metres down into the river before it wound its way towards Sungai Endau. On the left were Bukit Segongong and Anak Bukit Segongong. Across those peaks was the way back to base camp.

Rafting Down Sungai Endau

Sungai Endau, major river of the expedition area. (SLG)

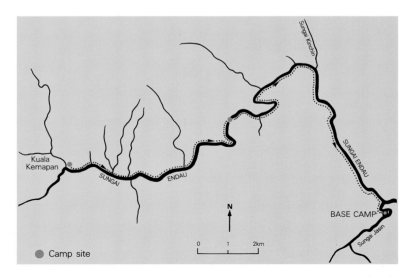

It's easier to get out and walk than to boat through the rapids. (HHH)

In September 1985, a three-day survey of the riverscape, water quality and vegetation of the Sungai Endau was made by a team from Universiti Pertanian Malaysia, who drifted down the Endau to Kuala Jasin in a rubber raft. The 15 kilometre journey was not only educational but adventure-filled for the team. Lai Food See writes:

The Sungai Endau is excellent for nature lovers and adventure seekers, especially those who like canoeing, fishing or simply camping by the river. Apart from being pollution-free, the Endau is very varied, with long stretches of sandy river bed, short stretches of stony bed and relatively sluggish flow, interrupted by rapids and huge boulders.

Our journey began at the confluence of the Sungai Endau and Sungai Kemapan, where we were dropped by an RMAF Nuri helicopter. We were equipped with cameras, a video camera and instruments needed for the study. We had mapped out ten stations where water sampling was to be carried out and water quality, channel width, depth and flow velocity measured.

Because of the dry weather at this time of the year, the water flow was gentle and the currents not excessively turbulent. But we could imagine the erosive force during the annual flood when the water level might rise by another two metres or more. Evidence of flood levels could be seen all along the river — logs and driftwood sat precariously on large boulders which were more than a metre above the water level at the time of our visit.

We camped for the first night where the helicopter had left us, and set off next morning. After drifting about two kilometres from Kuala Kemapan, we had to drag the boat for about 100 metres, trying to keep our balance because of abundant slimy algae on the rocky river bed.

The six major rapids along this stretch were exciting and could be treacherous. To avoid unnecessary risks, we stopped at each rapids to decide on the best possible route across. At each, we had our share of slippery adventure, and each of us took a fall now and then. At one bad stretch, two of our cameras fell in the river.

In the afternoon, after a furious storm, we reached a spectacular 400 metre stretch of giant boulders. We were relieved to get out of the boat to figure the best way through. After more than 45 minutes of manoeuvring, we got into navigable waters again. Amid this excitement we stopped at some points to examine the mass of rocks protruding from the river bed and found them to be well smoothed by the powerful action of the water. We camped for the second night by a narrow sandy beach immediately beyond this stretch.

Just after heavy rain, the rafters come to a river of giant boulders.(LFS)

Water quality was measured at ten sites along the Endau. (LFS)

End of journey: reaching the rapids at Kuala Jasin. (LFS)

A small boat to tackle a big river. (LFS)

Routine sampling resumed the next morning at the camp site. The water level had risen by 20 centimetres because of the storm. Our water samples did not indicate any substantial change in turbidity, indicating good quality water. At the same time and for a brief moment we witnessed a beautiful scene, with the early morning sun shining against a forest backdrop while the mist evaporated from the river.

Our mood changed after the Sungai Endau and Sungai Kinchin confluence: the river flow became sluggish and the riverscape less scenic. The forest on either side of the river was more disturbed.

However, two major rapids broke the monotony before the journey's end. Again, we had to decide on the best route across — the drop in the gradient was so clear. We had to unload the rubber raft partially to drag it across the shallow rocky bed. We collected the final set of data at station 10, just before the Sungai Jasin meets the Sungai Endau.

The journey had been fascinating. Aside from the excellent riverscape, we also found plenty of animal tracks along the sand banks — wild boar and tapir being the most common. Familiar echoes of the gibbon occasionally broke the silence. Along some stretches of the river, bamboo grew profusely. Small herbaceous plants were common in places — a pretty sight as they seemed to await the coming monsoon.

Up The Kinchin

Rapids on the Kinchin slow the journey. **(RA)**

A journey up the Sungai Kinchin was made in two boats to assess whether it would be justifiable to mount a larger-scale study of the Ulu Kinchin area. Dr Kiew Bong Heang took note of the flora and fauna while Dr Idris Mohamad studied the geology of the area. Dr Kiew writes:

Much of the forest around Sungai Kinchin was similar to that near base camp. But we did encounter some of Endau-Rompin's unique plants. Our survey showed Sungai Kinchin is a blackwater river, but however far we travelled we never reached the source of this peaty water.

The two boats, which we hired with their owners, proceeded up the Sungai Endau and we soon encountered our first major rapids, the Sungai Jasin rapids. The water was swift and white. Our Orang Hulu boatmen directed their boats into a channel where four men hauled them up, one by one. Every foot gained was sustained by the fifth man hanging on to the rope at the prow. Slowly and gradually the boats were hauled up.

A short cruise and we were at the next major rapids, where the whole tedious process was repeated. Once above the rapids, we were off to Kuala Kinchin without further trouble. We passed by a huge deep pool known as Lubok Buaya, which a white crocodile is believed to inhabit. Idris and his student Din were considered very brave — some Orang Hulu from Kampung Peta thought them foolhardy — to have swum across it on one of their earlier exploratory trips of the area. We stopped at Kuala Kinchin for lunch. The forest had been logged over and at this time of the day little animal or bird activity was observed.

The Sungai Endau at this point was well over 50 metres wide with greenish waters. Sungai Kinchin was 20 metres wide at its mouth, was slow-flowing and had peaty water the colour of well-brewed tea. The peaty water of Sungai Kinchin was totally diluted by the waters of the Sungai Endau and no trace of its brown water was detected downstream.

After lunch, we proceeded up the Sungai Kinchin. Soon it began to rain heavily. We had to continuously bail water out of the bottom of the boat and motored on, stopping only to refuel the engine. By 4.30 pm we arrived at our first rapids on Sungai Kinchin. After an hour of hauling our boat we passed a huge boulder known as Batu Labi-labi or Turtle Rock among the Orang Hulu, because of its flat top. The boats were steered to the side of the left bank and we climbed out to pitch camp just above Kuala Gerugal. We camped here for the next three nights. The forest had likewise been logged and looked similar to that near base camp.

While we built camp and prepared dinner, an elephant could be heard snapping trees and branches some distance away. We settled down to sleep to the chirping of crickets and grasshoppers. A chorus of lowland forest birds, cicadas and gibbons woke us from a restful sleep. After breakfast, we got ready for our day's excursion. Idris, Din and I set off to explore Sungai Gerugal. The river started off as a shallow muddy stream overgrown with pandan which made it difficult to walk. We cut a trail along the bank through the forest. A couple of hundred metres upstream it became sandy and rocky in places. We walked along the river bed so that we would not have to hack our way through the forest, and to avoid the leeches.

About half an hour later we came across some orange plastic tapes, which led us to an abandoned camp site. A message on one of the tapes said the Geological Survey of Malaysia had been in the area in 1980. We proceeded upriver and found it growing narrower and more rocky as we headed towards the source. By noon we were climbing up small waterfalls and scrambling over boulders. The rocks along the course of the river were mainly rhyolite, a type of volcanic rock also found around base camp. Faults in the rocks were observed and Idris and Din took some readings with their compasses to determine alignment and angles of dip. We did not climb high enough to reach the expected sandstone layer, and turned back at 2.30 pm because it was threatening to rain.

While Idris and Din were studying the rocks, I was collecting mosses along the river banks. I also collected some herbaceous plants, including two which might be new to science. Indeed, one turned out to be a new species of *Loxocarpus* in the African violet family. Most of the vegetation was similar to the forest near base camp. As we climbed up the slope we noticed the umbrella palm growing along the river banks.

Our return journey would have been uneventful had we

Each stretch of the Kinchin varies. **(TV3)**

retraced our steps. Feeling adventurous, we had decided to cut across to Sungai Anak Gerugal then on to Sungai Endau in a straight line across the forest. I was keen because this would allow me to look for signs of animals and study the vegetation in the forest. With Idris reading the compass, we crossed a low ridge and hit the Sungai Anak Gerugal without much trouble. We crossed another ridge, and came to some flat land and emerged on an old logging track. According to the compass and map, we could reach our destination by following a small stream, downriver. We found the stream and followed it, apparently upstream, and were soon back at the log bridge, where we had started! So we followed the stream again and after an hour's walk, cut across a low ridge to emerge on the bank of Sungai Endau opposite the camp where our boatman was waiting to ferry us back to camp.

The next morning the scientific party decided to explore Hill 750 behind the camp. The climb up the hill started off with lowland forest and ended with a fan palm forest like that found on top of Gunung Janing Barat. The rocks on the hill were mainly rhyolite ending with a thin layer of sandstone on top.

From the top of the hill we descended to a stream marked on the map. We plunged down the northern side to encounter an almost vertical slope, which we had to negotiate by grasping every available tree. The stream was dry and the rocks did not prove interesting either.

After following the stream for some distance we decided to cut back up the ridge again and returned to camp. We came across a pair of gibbons and signs of wild boar but little else, and only heard calls of a variety of lowland birds.

The next day, we set off in the boat for a bit of fishing and stopped at Kuala Genut to visit an abandoned tin mine in the middle of the forest. The trail that led to the mine

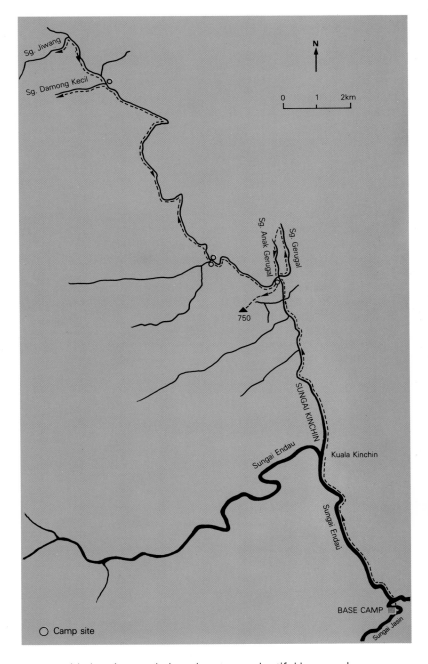

○ Camp site

was a wide logging track. Leeches were plentiful here and chased us wherever we went. The tracks of wild boars, tapir and a huge tiger were also to be seen. We half ran and half walked to the abandoned mine partly to avoid the leeches and partly in fear of the tiger.

Idris found some pieces of marble in the vicinity of the mine and we returned swiftly to the boat to avoid running into the tiger. We then proceeded up river. The logged forest was soon replaced by pristine lowland dipterocarp forest with huge trees. Proceeding further upstream we came to a dark and sinister-looking pool called Lubok Seluar (Pool of Trousers). According to an old Orang Hulu legend, the pool was so named because lots of trousers were found hanging on the bushes nearby. They apparently belonged to swimmers who had failed to emerge from the pool. No one knew what happened to them. It was suggested that they were drowned by the water spirit.

The journey up river was no easy task. After numerous rapids and shallow sections, we arrived at a two-metre waterfall. We were to haul our boat up a side channel. Having got the boat above the fall we took a rest. I then noticed some begonias growing on a sheltered damp rock face. I had been asked to look out for begonias, which had not been found so far in the Endau river system. Here was a very localised population of begonias. Perhaps they would be new to science? I collected a good representative sample only to be told later that it was the commonest and most widespread Malaysian species.

We continued upriver, stopping at Kuala Temakong for lunch, then motored for two hours to arrive at a section of the river with vertical rock banks, called Batu Dinding, Stone Wall.

Motoring further, we arrived at an old Orang Hulu camp site where we camped. It was a short distance away from the confluence of the Sungai Damong Kecil. The next day, the scientific party set off up the Sungai Damong Kecil behind the camp. Like the Sungai Gerugal, it was flat and covered with pandan at the confluence, gradually becoming sandy and rocky as it flowed down Gunung Jiwang. Towards its source small waterfalls and rapids became common. A new species of *Codonoboea* in the African violet family, which also grows on Gunung Janing, was collected here. The rock type was rhyolite.

The following day we travelled up river as far as we could by boat. The river was much more shallow and we had to push the boat more frequently and for longer distances. We got to Sungai Jiwang and waded up to look at the rocks and vegetation. Sungai Jiwang was easily the cleanest river I have seen. The water was crystal clear despite our wading.

A short distance up Sungai Jiwang we hit a shallow stretch of river more than 100 metres long. Tired and having had enough of hauling boats for one day, we turned back. The Sungai Kinchin at this point was still peaty with clear side streams joining it. The source of the peaty water must be well up Gunung Lesong.

The next morning we broke camp after a quick breakfast and set off down the river. We hoped to be back at base camp before dark. The journey down was much faster and many of the rapids could be traversed without getting out of the boat. By 2 pm we were at Kuala Kinchin again. With some difficulty we manoeuvred the boat down the two rapids on Sungai Endau and arrived at Kuala Jasin and base camp two hours later.

In September 1985, Shaharin Yussof and Tunku Mohd. Nazim Yaacob hiked from Kampung Selai, an Orang Hulu village in the south-west, to the heart of Endau-Rompin. The area is one of the few "wild" refuges left in Johor. In five days they covered 37 kilometres, or 18.4 kilometres as the hornbill flies. Below is an account of their adventure.

We had planned to head north-east over Gunung Tiong (1,015 metres), across a high level plateau we called "trackless wastes" to arrive at a large waterfall near the start of Sungai Jasin, and follow the river down to base camp.

Our two-man expedition set off from Batu Pahat in a borrowed four-wheel drive vehicle for Kampung Selai where the village headman sent some boys to show us the trail up Gunung Tiong.

After crossing the Selai in their boat, the boys led us through the forest and up the hill on paths used by rattan collectors. It was pouring with rain. When the paths ended, our guides left us, indicating the direction we should take.

Following a natural route we came across a salt lick with sambar deer and pig tracks. Above this point, the slopes became steeper and the trees shorter. After spending a night on a bamboo bed, we had to climb a few vertical rock faces before we reached the ridge top. This was a boggy place with thick peat, tall sedges and pandans in places. It was also covered in animal tracks. Sambar deer, pig, tapir and elephant all came up this 1000 metre mountain: why, we could not guess.

Navigating down mountains is never as easy as going up and like an elephant before us, we began our descent into the wrong valley and were forced to make a difficult traverse around and through thick bamboo, bertam and rattan. We passed a stand of *Cyathea* tree ferns, which are not common in Johor, and saw our first umbrella palms, *Johannesteysmannia altifrons*.

At 555 metres, we disturbed a group of pigs rooting around a salt lick. All the tracks here were of pigs and deer; tapir did not seem to be attracted. We were led on by the sound of a stream below for a much needed drink and wash.

From the salt lick we followed elephant trails to the north-east up a hill we called Bukit Tongkat Ali because, undisturbed, the well-known plant *Eurycoma longifolia* grew all around. We found argus pheasant dancing-grounds, and heard the cocks calling at a distance. A group of wreathed hornbills ponderously flew below us on the mountain side and far to the north a gibbon pair announced their presence.

Camp 2 was on umbrella palm leaves beside the pathway. A group of raptors, possibly Honey-buzzards, flew

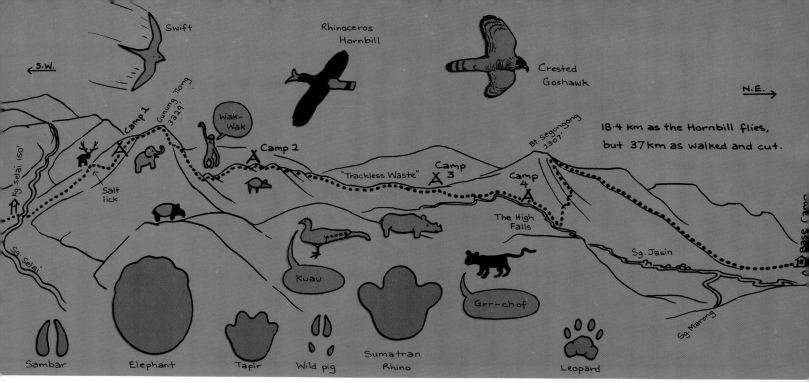

Swift

Rhinoceros Hornbill

Crested Goshawk

← S.W.

N.E. →

Camp 1

Gunung Tiong 3329'

Wak-Wak

Camp 2

Kg Selai 150'

Salt lick

"Trackless Waste"

Camp 3

Bt Segongong 1307'

Camp 4

18.4 km as the Hornbill flies, but 37km as walked and cut.

The High Falls

Sg. Jasin

Base Camp

Sg. Selai

Kuau

Grr-chof

Sg. Marong

Sambar   Elephant   Tapir   Wild pig   Sumatran Rhino   Leopard

by. That night we realised quite how vulnerable we were this deep in the forest. The previous afternoon we had opened up an old trail and in our footsteps followed a tapir with her calf. That night, before the moon rose, to her surprise and our terror she almost blundered into our tent. She took off crashing into the undergrowth to leave the baby squealing and us shivering. We had been woken by the noise and thought elephants were about to stomp through the camp. Twenty minutes later the squealing stopped so we hoped baby was reunited with mother.

We had been keeping to high ground where we could, but eventually we had to go down to the area we called "the trackless wastes". From aerial photographs the area is featureless with a low uniform tree cover. But it turned out to be neither trackless nor a waste. Coming down from Camp 2, the hill forest gave way to thicker undergrowth and climbers. We went through a few fan-palm groves on table-top ridges. From these ridges we descended into wetter and thicker forest below. *Licuala* palms grew here and so did thick bertam, and the canopy of the woody trees was only about ten metres high. This forest looked similar to the swampy riverside forest along the Sungai Sedili in coastal Johor. Pigs and elephants had made random paths and we also came across some rhinoceros tracks: as large as a spread hand with toe-lobes. The tracks were not as deep as those of an elephant and much bigger than those of a tapir. We kept on a bearing of north-north-east, following game trails when they coincided or else blazing our own trail until we intersected the Sungai Jasin.

Finding a site for Camp 3 was difficult on this swampy ground so we selected a small sand-bank by the river. As we approached we heard a sound familiar in the zoo. It was the sort of half cough and half hiss which a leopard makes when it is disturbed. Pigs had been rooting near the sand-

bank. Perhaps the leopard was expecting them back. We made a smoky fire that night.

We were 350 metres up here on this plateau but it was very warm. At dusk and dawn kijang barked and in the night the nightjars called. Leeches were active here as well.

About two hours down river from Camp 3, we came across an old Orang Hulu camp on a high bank of the river. Pelawan trees grew by the river bank and the edge of the water was fringed with ferns. We could hear the roar of the Buaya Sangkut falls in the distance. The Sungai Jasin was quite broad at this point and it meandered slowly through forest of increasing stature. Following one such stretch, which will one day become an ox-bow lake, we walked in almost a complete circle! Just before the waterfalls, the river picked up speed as it entered a narrow gorge. The roar of the falls was like an irresistible lure that led us on but the topography forced us to traverse a steep slope quite high above and out of sight of the river. Eventually we made our way down through the fan-palms and rengas trees to a deserted camp and the falls at Buaya Sangkut. Apart from a monitor lizard sun-bathing on a rock, we had the falls to ourselves. We swam in the pools above the falls and spent a long time just standing on the top watching the plunging water. We were not the first from the expedition to reach the site, but we reached it from a route no one else had taken before.

Unable to follow the river any further, and used to travelling by compass and parang, we wasted a whole morning making our own trail up Bukit Segongong before we realised it would have been easier to follow the expedition-cleared trail from Buaya Sangkut to base camp. Five hours later, in the pouring rain we arrived.

exciting
DISCOVERIES

exciting discoveries

Botanists found many new species of plants along the streams and on the nearby hills in Endau-Rompin. Three new trees were found, one of them a wild mangosteen. Others were new records for the country. Eight new herbs included white and purple flowered members of the African violet family, and a new *Dischidia* or ant-plant. Two mosses *Sematophyllum microcladioides* and *Chaetomitrium beccarii* were first records for Peninsular Malaysia, and in the rivers were found a new species of alga and 37 species of tiny diatoms, aquatic plants each encapsulated in a box-like shell, reported for the first time in Peninsular Malaysia.

The most spectacular of the new plant discoveries was the fan palm so characteristic of the ridges and hill tops. In places this palm, named *Livistona endauensis* by botanists, dominated the forest; on the plateau of Gunung Janing Barat it formed more than one third of all the growing trees. A great deal of discussion amongst scientists and visitors centred on this palm. Why was it so common in some places but rare in others? Was it gradually spreading downhill, or retreating to its hilltop strongholds? How fast did it grow, and what was its role in the functioning of the forest?

Many of Endau-Rompin's unique vegetation types were thought to be associated with poor soils. On Gunung Janing Barat swampy heath forest was confined to a waterlogged patch of white clay soil where nutrients are scarce. The pitcher plants there could supplement their diet by catching and digesting insect victims. Ant-plants of two main types either provided space in their flask-shaped leaves for ants to nest, sending roots into the nutritious material the ants brought into the leaves, or else enabled ants to live within their hollow tubers.

Elsewhere on the hilltop plateaux, botanists argued, only the *Livistona* fan palms could grow on the shallow soils over sandstone rocks. The big trees of other species could gain a place only where deeper cracks in the rock beneath, gave a better foothold and a better soil. Many trees on the plateau sent roots snaking up adjacent palm trees, again perhaps in search of extra nutrients trapped amongst the fronds.

It had been known for many years that in this part of eastern Johor a number of plant species are shared with Sarawak. An example, added in 1985, was the small tree *Rothmannia kuchingensis*. During the expedition, it became clear that this similarity extended to some of the forest types, notably the heath forest and its more extreme form the padang or open bog vegetation of Padang Temambong. Heath forests of this type are even better developed in Borneo. Within these heath forests the particular communities of birds in Borneo and in Johor are similar. And of course the bearded pig is one of the more striking mammals which Johor and Borneo share.

Amongst the smaller animals, a new species of trapdoor spider was found living in silk-lined burrows along the river banks. A new frog fell into the hands of an unsuspecting scientist, and a new crab was discovered living inside the cups of pitcher plants. Several of the fish found were rarities. Forest grasshoppers were, for the first time, found feeding on fungal spores and acting as dispersal agents for the fungi. New moths await description, while ants and wasps are still being studied. What is probably the third Malaysian record of the hairstreak butterfly *Hypochrysops coelisparsus* came from the flood-prone island, Pulau Jasin, where its caterpillars are likely to feed on the ferns which are so abundant there. These ferns include *Dipteris conjugata*, normally a montane plant but here growing less than 50 metres above sea level. This was not the only example of a plant from the mountains growing at exceptionally low altitudes at Endau-Rompin.

Evidently this cluster of hills topped by sandstone has served as a centre for the origin and evolution of unique species, and for the development of distinctive ecological communities such as the swampy heath forest, the fan palm forest and the padang.

Fan Palm New To Science

The fan palm is a species new to science. It is endemic to the Ulu Endau area so it was named *Livistona endauensis*.

Related palms are found on other hills, like Cameron Highlands and on Gunung Tahan in the state of Pahang and on Bukit Bauk in the state of Terengganu. The species in Endau-Rompin is not only restricted to a small area, but also seems to have special habitat requirements. Only on hill tops, on shallow soils over sandstone does it reach its maximum abundance and form forest. (A/ME)

Previous page
Main: Livistona endauensis. (HHH)
Inset: "Space Helmets", Alsomitra macrocarpa. ((SLG)

Plants On The Cliff

The sandstone rock faces which occur below the summit of mountains in the Endau-Rompin area are home to several rare and interesting plant species. Some grow nowhere else in the world, such as *Phyllagathis cordata.* (KR)

A Crab Inhabiting Pitcher Plants

One expedition participant, stopping for a well-earned rest in the swampy heath forest on Gunung Janing Barat, happened to look inside the cup of a pitcher plant, *Nepenthes ampullaria.* To his surprise a crab was sitting inside it!

A survey showed that any given pitcher never contained more than one crab. Many pitchers had nothing but a few mosquito larvae or dead insects inside, and a few had tadpoles.

Each of the crabs was about two centimetres across, mottled black and olive with bright red claws and a red belly. After referring back to older museum specimens, it was found that such crabs had in fact been found in other parts of Peninsular Malaysia, but until now they had never been recognised as something new. This new crab is now called *Geosesarma malayanum.* (KSN) (TS)

Endemic To Endau-Rompin

Phyllanthus watsonii (top right) grows along the Sungai Endau and its tributaries and nowhere else in the world. It is well adapted to the conditions where it lives on rapids and along the edge of the river, where it is often rooted in the water. Its root system is extensive and clings tenaciously to the substrate so that it is not dislodged by the floods. It branches from the base so that if its stems are broken off they are replaced by new ones.

Plants like *P. watsonii,* that can withstand strong water current and floods, are called rheophytes. The Sungai Endau has a wealth of rheophytes and an advantage of the Endau-Rompin expedition to scientists was the opportunity to study plants with such a highly restricted distribution. (HHH)

Tunku's Loxocarpus

Loxocarpus tunkui in the African violet family is a pretty plant with grey silky leaves and small purple flowers. It grows on rock faces beside streams. It was discovered in only two places, Sungai Kin-chin and Sungai Lemakoh, and is not known to grow anywhere else in the world. It has been named after Tunku Abdul Rahman, expedition patron. (RA)

Lost And Found In The Forest

Didissandra kiewii in the African violet family is the most stunningly beautiful herb at Endau-Rompin. Its trumpet-shaped deep purple flowers are black inside and its leaves are not only beautifully variegated but are crinkled too. The expedition leader, Dr. Kiew Bong Heang, stumbled on this new species in Sungai Selai when his group got lost on a trans-Endau expedition trek. He immediately recognised it as something special and brought specimens back. It is named for him. (KBH)

Caught On The Hop

An expedition scientist, walking back to base camp at dusk, was startled when a frog plopped down from the trees onto the ground in front of her. Pouncing on it, she brought it back with her. Herpetologist Dr Kiew Bong Heang found it to be a new species, intermediate in appearance between *Rhacophorus dulitensis* of Borneo and *R. promianus* of Peninsular Malaysia.

This dark green tree-living frog has now been named *Rhacophorus tunkui* in honour of YTM Tunku Abdul Rahman Putra Al-Haj. It joins two other animals so far newly discovered at Endau-Rompin, a trapdoor spider *Liphistius endau* and the crab *Geosesarma malayanum*. (KBH)

Riverside Beauty

Right under our noses at base camp on Sungai Jasin grows this new species in the African violet family, *Didymocarpus craspedodromus.* It not only grows on river banks but also on banks and rocks on Gunung Janing. It has since been recorded in Pahang as well. (KR)

Troublesome Taxonomy

Long study in the labora-
tory, visits to museums and
herbaria, and the borrowing
of other specimens may be
needed in order to describe
with confidence a new plant.
The profusely blooming *Schefflera* from the Jasin river basin
is one species which may be
new to science. *Schefflera*
varies so much in habit, and in
the size and shape of its leaf-
lets, and the species are so
closely related that it is difficult to distinguish them. More
work may be necessary on
this relative of the ginseng.(SLG)

Dweller on the Cliffs

The soft velvety leaves of
Didymocarpus falcatus quickly
advertised this plant as a
species new to science. Found
growing on the Janing escarp-
ment, the newly described *D.
falcatus* joins more than 50
others in the genus now known
from Peninsular Malaysia. A
number of these, like *D. falcatus,* are known from a single
locality. (KR)

The Copper Tree

A beautiful little tree by the
Sungai Jasin was found bearing copper-coloured leaves.
From specimens brought back
to the Forest Research Institute Malaysia it was found to
be a new species, now called
Schoutenia leprosula. It joins
a dozen other plant species
newly discovered by the expedition, and a dozen more
known only from Endau-
Rompin. (SLG)

Tree Roots That Climb

Roots do not normally grow upwards, let alone climb onto other tree trunks. Yet here in Endau-Rompin roots were frequently found zig-zagging their way to heights of up to eleven metres on the trunks of the fan-palm, *Livistona endauensis.*

These climbing roots were found to belong to such trees as pelawan, *Tristania merguiensis,* rengas, *Gluta aptera,* and bintangor, *Calophyllum* spp. which commonly occur together with the fan-palm.

In investigating the phenomenon on the Janing and Temambong plateaux, scientists from the Forest Research Institute Malaysia concluded that this climbing behaviour was the result of an interaction between the growth behaviours of both the palm trees and the roots.

As young palms develop a trunk, their rosette-like crown of leaves rises progressively higher from the forest floor, but the persistent bases of old fronds remain for a while on the palm trunk just below its crown. These old fronds trap a "jacket" of organic debris around the palm's trunk. Such debris, of course, provides the substrate for root growth.

This organic jacket on the palm trunk becomes gradually raised to higher levels as a young palm grows up. Thus the fine roots of other trees, which have grown into the organic debris, continue to grow, upwards, as the palm develops the spiral rows of leaf-bases on the palm trunk, and so develop a zig-zag structure.

There are few reports of upwardly growing roots anywhere in the world, and none previously on this particular mode of ascent onto palm trunks. (JD)

Ant Gardens

This was an exciting phenomenon new to Malaysia. Ant-gardens, previously documented in South America, are created by ants which carry the seeds of particular plants into their ant runways and nests where they germinate. It is thought the seeds of these species elicit the response in ants for carrying prey back to the nest. One such ant-garden plant is *Pachycentria main-gayi,* others include *P. constricta* and some *Dischidia* species. These plants, which are epiphytes, benefit because their seeds get an ideal place to germinate and become established. At one time it was thought that the swollen root of *P. maingayi* was nibbled hollow by the nesting ants. This is not so. More probably the root acts as a water storage organ. (JD)

(SY)

A Home In The Leaves

Dischidia major (often called by its old name *D. rafflesiana)* is an ant plant *par excellence*. Ant-plants are presumed to enjoy a symbiotic relation where both ants and plant benefit from the partnership. In the case of the ant, usually *Iridomyrmex* species, it keeps its broods in the flask-shaped leaves. For the plant, if its leaves are inhabited by ants, it produces roots which grow into the leaf cavity and presumably absorb nutrients from the debris deposited there by the ants. Ants also disperse the seeds. However, *D. major* can grow perfectly well without ants.

A new species of *Dischidia* was among the plants discovered at Endau-Rompin.

A Cone-bearing Epiphyte

Green land plants, the club-mosses bear no seeds and are most closely related to ferns. Though several small species are common on waste ground, *Lycopodium dalhousianum* is confined to the forest and impressively big. One of the largest club-mosses in the world, it is an epiphyte and at Endau-Rompin was found growing on the new palm *Livistona endauensis.* It is amongst the most attractive epiphytes, with long soft blue-green tassels. (SLG)

A Malaysian Grape

Members of one family, the obvious link between *Pterisanthes stonei* and the grape vine is their clambering habit. A closer look reveals similarities in the flowers and fruits, but those of *P. stonei* are borne on a strange, flattened red strap. This fruit-bearing strap changes from green to red as the fruits ripen. One of several Malaysian species, *P. stonei* was only known from three localities till its discovery at Endau-Rompin. (JD)

The Monkey's Head

Locally called "pokok kepala beruk" (monkey's head plant), *Hydnophytum formicarium* is a bizarre plant by any standard. It is an epiphytic shrub. This means that it grows on other plants without getting any food from the supporting plant. Its bizarre appearance is due to its swollen stem base (known as the hypocotyl) which is enlarged into a round brown structure, the "monkey's head". It is riddled with chambers in which ants live, and the plant obtains food from the debris brought in to these chambers by the ants. Equally important is the tuber's role in water storage.

Ant plants including this one were particularly common in selected forest types at Endau-Rompin, and were the subject of a special study. (JD)

Reservoir In The Trees

In the open and stunted padang vegetation, any plant may experience a water shortage in dry weather. Still more are those perched on exposed tree branches liable to suffer desiccation. Epiphytes like *Hydnophytum formicarium* and this *Pachycentria constricta* seem to have solved the problem by storing water in their swollen hypocotyl.

The hypocotyl at the base of the stem is tuberous and riddled with little tunnels. Once it was thought the tunnels might be dug out by the ants which live inside them. But it now seems they may be an adaptation by the plant to increase surface area. If there is a sudden shower water must be collected quickly, and any rain flowing into the tunnels could be absorbed through their walls. There is clearly a complex relationship between the plant, ants, nutrients and environment. (WKM)

The Diminutive Banana

Musa gracilis grows one to two metres tall and is the smallest wild banana plant in Peninsular Malaysia. An endemic species, it was thought to be very rare until it was found extensively in the Endau-Rompin area during the expedition. It has since been found to be common in Terengganu. It has potential as a garden plant as it is small, and its bananas are unusual in being almost white. In common with all wild bananas its fruits cannot be eaten because they are full of hard black seeds. (A/ME)

Buried Treasure

Fruits of the earth-fig *Ficus uncinata* were found in Endau-Rompin. Slender string-like runners grow out from the base of the tree's trunk, bearing bunches of red fruits. Unless disturbed they lie hidden under the forest litter, where perhaps small mammals like rats and mouse-deer eat them and so spread the seeds to new places. Found only in Peninsular Malaysia and Borneo, this earth-fig is one of a hundred Malaysian species and one of the world's thousand figs! (SLG)

The Admirable Palm

Many palm fruits are dull green or brown, but *Pinanga* and *Iguanura* often have brightly coloured red, yellow, or white or even glossy black fruits. Perhaps they are eaten by birds or mammals; they grow close to the ground and change colour as they ripen. Some are sweet. More observations are needed to confirm whether palm fruits like these are dispersed by animals.

After the expedition this was found to be a new species of palm similar to *Pinanga mirabilis.* Can you find the frog in this picture? (KR)

Space Helmets

These curious space helmets were first spotted on the heads of some Orang Hulu youngsters in Kampung Peta by a botanical team from the Forest Research Institute Malaysia. The helmets on examination turned out to be the shell of a fruit, large enough to fit the head once a portion for the face had been cut away. Not being able to identify the fruit in this condition, the botanists persuaded the children to lead them to the plant bearing the fruits. It was a large vine, growing to more than five metres high, clambering on a tree near the river in secondary forest. Numerous large green spherical fruits, ripening brown, dangled through the dense foliage. The vine was later identified as *Alsomitra macrocarpa,* a member of the gourd family.

A fully grown fruit is about the size of a coconut. When ripe it splits into three. Rapid drying sets in, releasing the seeds, which have a filmy transparent wing measuring about 12 centimetres from tip to tip. These seeds are dispersed by wind over long distances, and have even been picked up on the decks of schooners at sea off the Aru Islands. (SLG)

The Southern Element

Two plants of the genus *Euthemis* were found growing at Endau-Rompin. One of them, *E. leucocarpa,* is common throughout the country. The other, *E. minor,* is a shrub about two metres tall found along the Sungai Jasin and Sungai Endau. It is also present in the heath forests of the area. This plant had been thought extinct in Peninsular Malaysia.

Previously it was known from the islands of Singapore and obviously has a narrow geographical distribution. Several other plants have this same southern distribution sometimes referred to as the Riouw pocket. The Endau-Rompin area is very important conservation-wise to protect members of the southern flora. (KSN)

A Borneo Link

Rothmannia kuchingensis was found on Gunung Janing. Previously known only from Borneo, it now joins the small group of plants which provide a link between Johor and Borneo floras. Such disjunct distributions have provided botanists with insights into the past when climate and sea levels varied. (TS)

Kelesa

Considered endangered world-wide, the Kelesa, *Scleropages formosus* is a fine aquarium fish. The huge scales on its flanks resemble coins, especially in those individuals which are shiny. Different fish may be red, silver, grey or gold. The Kelesa is now becoming rare as a result of over-exploitation, and may soon face the threat of extinction. It was therefore good news to find this fish in one part of Endau-Rompin, but the location must be kept secret to protect it.

The Kelesa belongs to an ancient group of bony fishes now confined to fresh waters in the three main tropical regions of the world, South America, Africa and South-East Asia. One of its relatives, the Arapaima of the Amazon basin, is the largest fresh-water fish in the world. (*KSN)

Plants That Run

Most plants spread by means of their fruits, carried by animals or rolling down hill, or by branching from the base. The dwarf salak palm *Salacca minuta* at Kuala Kemapan was found sending out suckers, or runners. These runners sprout from one palm and loop over through the leaf litter, to branch into a new palm some feet away. A third of all Peninsular Malaysian palms grow in Endau-Rompin, and *S. minuta* is one of the area's three endemic palms. (SLG)

Traulia azureipennis. (KM)

Grasshoppers In The Forest

Most grasshoppers like to live in long grass, in clearings or along roadsides. Grass itself is one of their most important foods. Grasshoppers which live completely within the forest are special and rare. Though some grasshoppers with wings do survive in the forest, many of them are wingless.

Why do most forest grasshoppers not have wings? Perhaps one reason is the scarcity of food resources - leaf litter is not very nutritious and flying does take a lot of energy. So these insects may use the available energy for reproduction rather than flight. This idea is one of the many awaiting further study.

At Endau-Rompin one special wingless species was observed, *Sedulia specularia.* Its body is beautifully camouflaged like the colours of the mottled leaf litter, and to avoid detection, it stays absolutely still when threatened.

It is well adapted to feeding on the leaf litter which covers the forest floor. Leaf litter is rapidly broken down and decomposed by a variety of insects as well as by fungi. What is exciting is that *Sedulia* also eats fungi and the fungal spores it eats are not digested but are excreted. These spores can then germinate and infect new areas of leaf litter. So we have found a grasshopper which not only eats fungi but

Juvenile stage, or nymph, of an undentified bush cricket in the subfamily Phaneropterinae. (KM)

Bush cricket *Eumegalodon sp.* (KM)

Grasshopper *Sedulia specularia.* (KM)

Forest grasshopper *Althaemenes maculalutea.* (KM)

may also play an important role in the recycling of nutrients in the forest by spreading the fungi from place to place.

Another species, new to the Endau-Rompin area, was identified as *Althaemenes maculalutea.* Only one was found during three weeks of work. Like many forest insects, it is probably very scarce. This specimen had long wings, and a bulky prothorax like a bull's neck that made it look very threatening.

In open clearings one can often find more familiar species. This raises the question of how they got there in the first place. For example, how did *Traulia azureipennis*

find its way from grassland in the lowlands up to Padang Temambong at 700 metres? Rain forest grasshoppers are full of mysteries.

Bush crickets, close relatives of the grasshoppers, are also to be found in the forest. In fact, they are probably more common than grasshoppers in this habitat. But many are nocturnal, and to find them one has to go out armed with a strong flashlight to inspect shrubs and trees. Bush crickets have more surprising shapes than grasshoppers. *Eumegalodon* is a big name for a big cricket that looks like a nightmare. The elaborate projections on its prothorax behind the head may deter

predators from eating it. It is often found feeding on bamboo, which is tough, so the cricket needs its massive jaws to chew through the thick leaves. It is not averse to giving humans a quick nip either! In contrast to that ugly beast was a bush cricket of the most beautiful blue and black, spotted during a hike up to Padang Temambong. It was only a nymph, not fully adult, so its identity will remain unknown until an adult is discovered. If the Endau-Rompin forest disappears, perhaps this cricket will never be seen again.

A Home for Tadpoles

Pitcher plants are adapted to catch insects passively in their pitchers. The pitchers, which develop from the tips of leaves, produce nectar which attracts insects. They slip on the waxy rim and fall into the water inside. After they drown, enzymes in the water digest them and release nutrients that are absorbed by the wall of the pitcher. However, the enzymes cannot digest living creatures and several make their home there, including crabs, tadpoles and mosquito larvae.

At Endau-Rompin three sorts of pitcher plants grow in open areas such as Pulau Jasin and in swampy heath forest. The most handsome one is *Nepenthes rafflesiana,* which produces large purple ground-pitchers. (MG)

Swamp on the Hill Top

It is logical to look for swamps in the low-lying places where water gathers. At Endau-Rompin the places most often waterlogged were on hill tops! The shallow bowl of the Gunung Janing plateau supported a most unusual vegetation type, swampy heath forest rich in conifers, orchids and sedges. The variety of habitat within a small area adds enormously to the value of Endau-Rompin. (KR)

Down From The Mountains

In Endau-Rompin the fern *Matonia pectinata* is found only on Pulau Jasin and in the heath-forest. Elsewhere in the country it is found on isolated mountain summits and high ridges above 1,000 metres. The nutrient-poor soil conditions seem to have influenced its presence at very low altitudes in the expedition area. The small tree *Leptospermum flavescens* is another example of an otherwise montane plant occurring on Pulau Jasin.

There are many fossil ferns which have fronds like *Matonia,* dating from Mesozoic times. The family Matonaceae to which it belongs was then distributed even into the Arctic, but is now confined to isolated mountains in South-East Asia. (SLG)

Green Prawns

Translucent young prawns were found in every river and pool at Endau-Rompin. In a little pool below a cascade on the Sungai Zain, near the foot of Gunung Janing, was found a colony of green prawns. They were not new to science, but what was their correct name?

After a great deal of argument and detective work searching the literature, it was finally agreed they were *Atyopsis moluccensis,* a name which, printed on this page, is considerably longer than the owner. The opportunity was taken to make a study of the prawns, measuring each one with calipers. (DL)

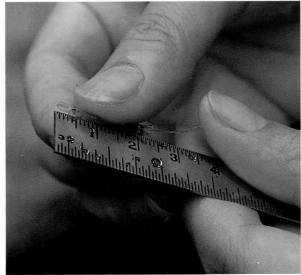

Walking Sticks

The walking-stick palm *Rhopaloblaste singaporensis* is one of the commonest undergrowth palms at Endau-Rompin. It is decorative and has great potential as an ornamental plant. The expedition area is rich in palms and 72 species in 20 genera were recorded, representing about one third of all palm species in Peninsular Malaysia. Some of these are extremely rare, such as the Endau rattan *Calamus endauensis,* which is only known from a single clump at Sungai Sempanong, Endau-Rompin. (SLG)

RHYTHMS
of the forest

rhythms of the forest

On a single walk into the forest many unusual plants can be seen, such as the fan palms and pitcher plants. Looking closer, trails of ants and termites, crickets, spiders and a host of other small creatures can be found on the tree trunks, or hidden amongst the leaf litter.

But only by repeated visits over a long period can we appreciate that the forest is an ever-changing landscape. There are many rhythms by day and by night, season by season, and year by year. An advantage to scientists of a full 13 months' work at Endau-Rompin was the chance to study and relate these changes one to another.

Above: More trees bear new leaves in February than in any other month. (LYK)

Previous page
Main: Green tree frog **Rana hosei.** (JD)
Inset, left: Single flowers emerge one by one from between the brilliant red bracts of a ginger **Zingiber** *inflorescence.* (A/ME)
Inset, right: Saturniid moth **Antheraea helferi,** *male.* (JD)

(MS)

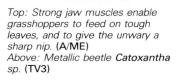

Top: Strong jaw muscles enable grasshoppers to feed on tough leaves, and to give the unwary a sharp nip. (A/ME)
Above: Metallic beetle *Catoxantha sp.* (TV3)

Top: Many of the largest forest insects, like this female grasshopper, are active only at night. (PG)
Above: Both flight and sudden long jumps are effective escape methods for insects. (JD)

Light And Dark

Being so close to the equator, changes in the forest between night and day are more obvious than the changes from season to season.

The forest by night seems very different from the same place by day. This is because two sets of animals call it home, one diurnal, the other nocturnal.

Early in the morning, before it is light, the calls of insects are joined by the cautious hooting of a male gibbon. Birds join in the dawn chorus: a cuckoo, then tree-babblers and a barbet. Only as the morning draws on do the female gibbons join in the duets with their respective males, their great crescendo of wails carrying far over the forest. Grasshoppers, crickets and cicadas add to the chorus.

It is during the morning that birds and many other animals are at their most active. After a long night the demands of the stomach must be satisfied, before the day becomes too hot. Caterpillars wind their way over twigs and under leaves, preparing themselves for adulthood. Those sun-lovers, the butterflies, can be seen hovering above and feeding from flowers in open areas of the forest.

By noon most of the activity has ceased, and even the green cicada is silent. Only in the late afternoon after the heat of the day has passed, is there a second burst of activity. Evening is a particularly rewarding time to watch birds from the top of the tree tower; a pair of wreathed hornbills might pass on their way to roost, a woodpecker tap briefly, or a cluster of minivets pause in the twigs a few feet away. As the sun begins to set, a rasping cicada heralds dusk. A Malaysian eared nightjar, *Eurostopodus temminckii,* high over the trees, invites us to "Drink-your-beer! Drink-your-beer!" And the first bat flitters past in search of its tiny insect prey.

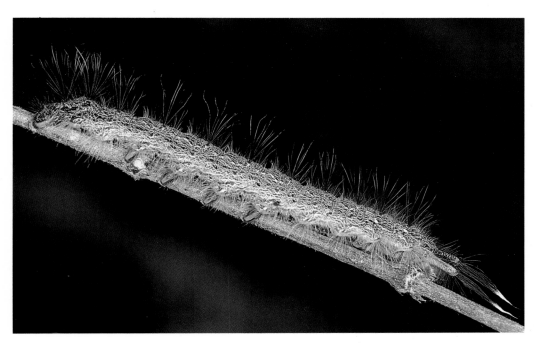

Top: Other insects rely on dull colouring to escape notice, and stinging hairs as a defence. (A/ME)
Above: Caterpillars active by day can be startlingly coloured to warn off predators. (A/ME)

Night has fallen but the forest is not asleep. Owls hoot and rats move warily amongst the leaf litter. High on a tree trunk, a whip-scorpion emerges from a crevice in search of food, while spiders and cockroaches add to the renewed activity. Along the river, frogs and toads produce all kinds of weird sounds — loud lowing like cows, bubbling like water being emptied from a bottle, blips, trills, whistles, and hoots. Now is the time to be out with a flashlight to catch the eyeshine of nocturnal creatures, and fix them momentarily in the beam of light. Close to base camp a nightjar resting on the trail is given away by the red reflection from its eye. Frogs and toads and spiders' eyes all shine back, yellow, red and green. The python, *Python reticulatus,* no longer sluggish, becomes a sleek hunter, joining those other hunters of the night, the tiger and the lithe panther.

Back in camp, moths of all kinds flutter round the lamps, and large beetles senselessly knock against the glass. A grey tree-rat, *Lenothrix canus,* which has made its home in the dried palm leaves of the camp roof, emerges to sit on a cross-beam. Overhead fly bats. Some of them swerve and twist to catch passing moths. Others fly more purposefully in the direction of a fruiting tree, whose ripe fruits perhaps are remembered from the night before, while still others drink nectar from night blooming flowers, the durian, *Durio zibethinus* and the putat, *Barringtonia* spp.

Top: Among the great variety of nocturnal life may be species new to science. (JD)
Right: **Graphium doson** *(Papilionidae), active by day.* (A/ME)
Centre: Hawk moth **Elibia dolichus.** (JD)
Far right: **Euthalia monina** *(Nymphalidae).* (A/ME)

Above: The subtle colouring of moths, and the under surface of butterflies, may be most important during the day, for it is the predator's own visual abilities, not those of the insect, which will determine how effective the camouflage is.

Top: Spiny-stomached spider
Gasteracantha sp.. (KR)
Above: A female huntsman spider,
of unidentified species, closely
guards her disc-like white package of
eggs under her body till the babies
hatch. (PG)
Right: Waiting for victims at the
water's edge is a successful
alternative to web-building. (JD)

Top: The "lantern" of the lantern-
bug **Fulgora** sp. does not light up,
and its function is unknown (KR)
Above: If disturbed by day, the
inflatable orange prothorax of this
longicorn grasshopper may deter
predators. (JD)

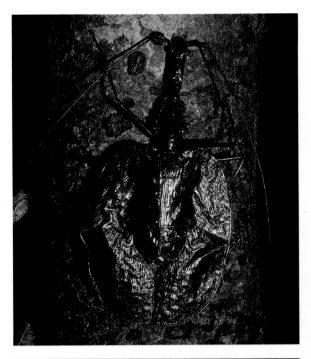

Top: Fiddle beetle **Mormolyce phyllodes.** (TS)
Centre: Forest cockroaches forage at night, and are well camouflaged by day. (TS)
Below: Sap-sucking bugs can be found at any time of year, and sometime in big concentrations in the canopy during leaf-flush. (JD)

Far right: After giving birth to her babies, a mother scorpion cares for them diligently. (TMNY)

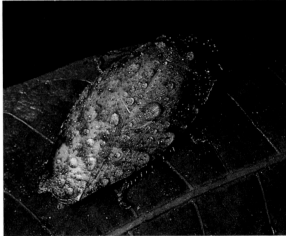

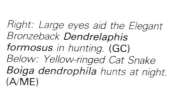

*Right: Large eyes aid the Elegant Bronzeback **Dendrelaphis formosus** in hunting. (GC)
Below: Yellow-ringed Cat Snake **Boiga dendrophila** hunts at night. (A/ME)*

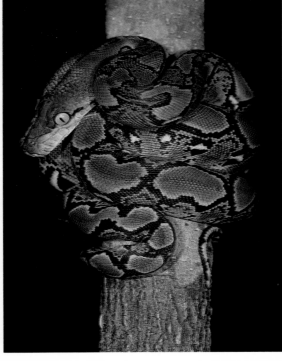

Active by night:
Top: Juvenile Reticulated Python
Python reticulatus. *(KR)*
Above: Grey tree rat **Lenothrix canus.**
(JD)
Right: Spotted-winged Fruit-bat
Balionycteris maculatus. *(GD)*

Most frogs are nocturnal and particularly noisy after rain.
Top: Malayan giant frog **Rana blythi** *form* **tuberculata.** *(KBH)*
Above left: Malaysian frog **Rana malesiana.** *(GD)*
Above right: Straight-ridged toad **Bufo parvus.** *(PG)*
Bottom left/ Main: Malayan house frog **Polypedates leucomystax.** *(GC) (TS)*

Leaf And Bud

Sources of nectar such as these are not available every night, for these trees have their own rhythms of flowering and fruiting. Although the forest at Endau-Rompin seems a place where trees continually bear fruit, each sort of tree has its distinctive cycle.

Endau-Rompin, because it is on the eastern side of Peninsular Malaysia, is strongly affected by the north-east monsoon. Most rain falls between about October and January during the intermonsoon changeover period, though the weather is so variable that floods can occur in almost any month. Studies of water levels at Endau-Rompin also demonstrated the lesser influence of the south-west monsoon in April and May. As in other parts of the country seasonal changes in rainfall, or the amount of cloud and sunshine, which follow a similar pattern, are related to the two flowering seasons of the trees.

Some plants like *Curculigo* and *Grewia* flower almost continuously, bearing buds, flowers and fruits simultaneously throughout the year. Others may flower once a year or twice a year at predictable intervals. The fan palm *Livistona endauensis* apparently flowers around February to March. Some of the largest trees may only flower once in three to five years, such as keruing, *Dipterocarpus* species. A major flowering season of the big trees occurred at Endau-Rompin in April to May, with their fruits ripening in July to August. For some, such as petai, *Parkia* spp., there was a second, less well-marked, flowering season about September to October, resulting in ripe fruits at the turn of the year. This is the classic pattern so well known for durian, with its one major and one minor fruiting season.

Flowers of one kind or another can be found at any time, and the seasons

Top: *Uncaria cordata* flowers near the forest edge. (SLG)
Above left: Putat *Barringtonia macrostachya* in flower, a plant pollinated by bats. (KBH)
Above right: *Thottea grandiflora* on the Janing ridge: a clear rhythm of leaf and flower production. (SLG)

Top right: *Swintonia penangiana* fruiting next to the tree tower. (SLG)
Bottom right: Sporangia of *Lycopodium cernuum* may be seen at any season. (KR)

Right: Maingay's Ginger **Nicholaia maingayi.** (HHH)
Centre: **Nauclea officinalis** in flower at Sungai Jasin. (SLG)
Below: **Ixora lobbii.** (A/ME)

Left: Flower heads of the ginger *Achasma megalocheilos* are often colonised by tiny biting ants. (A/ME)
Below: *Ploiarium alternifolium.* (A/ME)

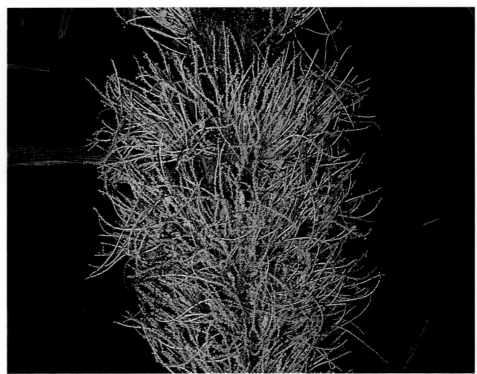

*Above: Mempisang **Polyathia** is a
large genus, with 10 or 15 sorts
often found growing within a single
area. Their habit of flowering on the
trunk is shared with several
understorey trees. (JD)*
*Top right: **Baccaurea parvifolia,**
like a few other understorey trees,
flowers round the base of its trunk.
(SLG)*
*Right: The male tree of **Baccaurea
parvifolia** looks more bedraggled
than the female. (TS)*

of the forest are statistical ones, when rather more flowers or rather fewer than usual can be found. The colourful inflorescences of *Ixora*, *Hanguana* and gingers, all of them understorey plants at Endau-Rompin, can be found throughout the year. The prickly bertam palm *Eugeissona tristis*, found so abundantly during the journeys described in Chapter 4, is perhaps another of these perpetual flowerers, pervading the air with a curious scent of yoghurt. Many of the trees, however, adhere more strictly to a seasonal pattern, like penarahan, *Knema furfuracea*, the black durian *Coelostegia borneensis*, and the false rengas tree *Swintonia penangiana* overhanging the tree tower, all of which were bearing fruit in September. Each of these plants must be responding to a different combination of cues from seasonal changes in the light and weather.

Trees in full flower may be beautiful, but sometimes they are overshadowed by a much more showy display of coloured young leaves, that in a few days transform a green tree crown into a startling white, pink or red. It is when these succulent young shoots are available that, in response to the sudden supply of food, colourful bugs appear in great numbers.

The seasons of the forest plants affect the birds too. Many kinds of smaller birds like the Blue-winged Leafbird *Chloropsis cochinchinensis*, could find, in the fruits of the senduduk *Melastoma malabathricum* along the logging tracks of Endau-Rompin, a source of food throughout the year. Fruit-eaters of the tree tops, Thick-billed Pigeons *Treron curvirostra*, on the other hand, must needs make extensive journeys in search of suitable ripe fruits.

*Top: The broad strap-shaped leaves of **Hanguana malayana** are a common sight in low-lying spots, but flowering or fruiting plants are unusual. (A/ME)*
*Left: Bertam fruits **Eugeissona tristis** grow in an erect cluster several feet tall. (A/ME)*

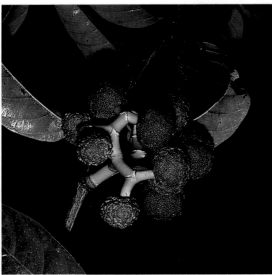

Top left: Fruits of **Dysoxylum** sp.
(SLG)
Above: **Poikilospermum,** a climber.
(RA)
Top right: **Pandanus** fruit at Gunung
Janing. (KR)
Right: Penerahan **Knema
furfuracea.** (SLG)

Above: The brilliant colours of **Coelostegia borneensis** fruits, when split, surely act as a signal to animals. (SLG)
Right: **Coelostegia borneensis** in fruit in Kuala Kemapan in September. (WKM)
Left: **Melodinus orientalis.** (SLG)

Right: Blue-winged leafbirds
Chloropsis cochinchinensis found
plentiful fruits of senduduk
Melastoma malabathricum along
logging tracks. (MS)
Below: Buff-rumped woodpecker
Meiglyptes tristis. (MS)
Facing page: Thick-billed pigeons
Treron curvirostra seen every
morning in the bare trees opposite
base camp. (MS)

The Eternal Forest

To many of us the life of a forest may seem static, but our time frame is different from that of, say, a seraya tree *Shorea curtisii*, which may live for 750 years. The rains and the floods bring down and sweep away the weak, the dying and the dead. A gap is torn in the forest, letting in the bright sunshine; seedlings and young trees struggle upwards to fill the gap before it closes. So the cycle continues, one species replacing another but ever maintaining the equilibrium of the forest.

Sunlight and water are the two major powers which drive this cycle. Both affect the rhythms of flowering amongst the forest trees, and both are related to that other feature of Endau-Rompin, its rivers. Being in the humid tropics where temperature and evaporation are constantly high, river flow closely follows the rainfall regime. The rivers in Endau-Rompin experience a double pulse, with two distinct peaks of high water resulting from the south-west and north-east monsoons.

Wet And Dry

On the wetter eastern side of Endau-Rompin there are about 3400 millimetres (130 inches) of rain each year, of which over half falls from October to January. Further into the forest to the west, total rainfall is only about two thirds as great. Apart from that lost directly again by evaporation, this water drains out by the major rivers the Endau and Selai and, in Pahang, the Rompin river. The expedition to Endau-Rompin discovered that the discharge from the Endau averages 220 cubic metres (48,000 gallons) every second. This rate of discharge varies, however, according to the amount of rain, and almost half of the total discharge occurs from October to January.

Top: Tree-fall gaps vary enormously in extent, depending on the violence of the storm responsible as well as the damage caused by the falling trees. (KSN)
*Above: **Livistona endauensis** seedling, Gunung Janing Barat.* (WKM)

Above: Young rattan (LC)
Far left: The most southerly record of the bamboo **Gigantochloa ligulata.** (WKM)
Left: Saplings grow very slowly till they find a break in the canopy. (JD)

Above: Once or twice a year, riverside plants can expect to be swept by floods. **(KSN)**
Right: Camps built by Orang Hulu on shingle banks need only be temporary, since they are used as collection centres for rattan and other forest products. **(TV3)**

In view of the vast area, the streams and rivers not only behave according to the weather changes from time to time but are also influenced by the terrain of Endau-Rompin. Following the beginnings of a stream right down to the valley bottom and flood plain, there is a gradual change in the character of the river system.

In their upper reaches the streams have steep gradients and flow in narrow steep-sided valleys. Many of these streams were studied at Endau-Rompin: Sungai Zain and Sungai Bong not far from the base camp, and the tributaries of the Kemapan and Kinchin described in Chapter 4. The flow of water in these streams is almost always swift and torrential. Waterfalls result from abrupt changes in the gradient of the stream beds.

Along their central sections the rivers have a flood plain and much less steep valley sides. The gradient of the river bed is less than that upstream but is by no means insignificant. Water flow in this section can be swift in parts and sluggish in others. Those who visited the base camp recall the way in which rapids near Kuala Jasin blocked progress of the boat, so the last stretch into camp had to be made on foot.

In its lowest reaches the river runs over a broad plain with very gently sloping sides. The gradient of the stream is very slight and river flow is usually sluggish. This is the form the Sungai Endau takes downstream of Kampung Peta, where it meanders across almost level ground towards the sea.

From youth to maturity, therefore, each river itself represents a vastly prolonged cycle of evolution.

Storms and seasonal high waters can scour away sandbars and beaches. With receding flows, silt and sand transport from upstream can quickly build them up again. When

available, the larger of these sandbars are used as camp sites for fishing expeditions along the Endau by the people of Kampung Peta. Gravel bars too are frequently seen during dry weather when the river level is low. Although they seem stable, the gravel can also be subject to transportation downstream by floods. Along gentler tracts, erosion and re-deposition of sand and silt occur naturally, and this influences the growth of plants there. Depending on the flood volume, especially during the monsoon months, such colonies of plants can be swept away entirely. It is because of this natural selective pressure that riverside plants have over the millenia developed their adaptations of tough stem, clinging root and slender leaf.

Endau-Rompin is exceptional only in the number of its riverside plants which are endemic to the area. The yearly rhythm of floods and low water is responsible for far more than immediately meets the eye.

Above: Flooding along the banks of the Sungai Marong affects the riverside vegetation. (JD)

Above/Right: Within a few minutes rain can transform the stream at Padang Temambong from a trickle to a broad sweep of water. **(SY) (SLG)**

the
EXPEDITION
in swing

the expediton in swing

I t took several months from the time it was launched in June 1985 for the expedition to get going in top gear. Even as the first group of scientists and volunteers went in to the forest, there were funds to be raised and transport arrangements to be made.

In the very beginning, base camp comprised sleeping quarters for ten people under a plastic roof, with a working area for scientists, a kitchen and a food store. From this basis additions were made as more and more people came to Endau-Rompin. The sleeping quarters were expanded to accommodate 50 people, and then an annexe had to be built for an extra ten. A fire in the kitchen, which burnt the roof, provided the impetus to enlarge and improve the design. A big dining area was roofed over, next to a simple 'laboratory' (two tables and a shelf). With more experience the architecture was continually improved, and eventually a separate house was built for Sangka, a full-time employee from Kampung Peta to stay with his family, sleeping quarters for two MNS staff members, and a clinic.

The building of the dormitory was a fine example of local ingenuity. The main vertical beams, stripped tree trunks, supported a long gable roof which sloped from 4 metres at its ridge down to one metre at the two long sides. This was thatched with the giant leaves of daun payong, *Johannesteysmannia altifrons,* a palm which grew abundantly at Endau-Rompin and which proved far cooler than the plastic sheets used earlier. Sets of wooden rails about one metre off the ground ran the

Left: Base camp was set in logged forest next to the Sungai Jasin. (SLG)

Previous page
Main: Hauling over the rapids on Sungai Endau. (HHH)
Inset, left: Arriving at Kuala Jasin. (CSE)
Inset, right: Base Camp 1985. (TS)

Top: Freshly cut leaves brought in from the surrounding forest. (LYK)
Middle: Splits in the leaf midribs form a simple method of overlap and attachment. (KSN)
Bottom: The leafy roof is quick to make and quick to repair. (WKM)

length of the dormitory. Stretch a piece of canvas between two poles, place this stretcher on the rails, and a bed is made. The kitchen was equipped with a kerosene oven, gas rings and a sink, in addition to all the pots and kettles and pans and plates and spoons and cups and knives. There was even a generator for the lights at night, a pump to draw water from the river, and flush toilets! A five star camp!

Running of the camp was placed on the shoulders of Tang Fook Leong, the camp manager, known to everyone as Leong. He was later joined by Heah Hock Heng as education officer/ cook. They and their visitors were watched with surprised but friendly interest by the residents of Kampung Peta. Unused to such numbers, and sometimes puzzled by the reasons for studying obscure little animals and plants, the Kampung Peta people nevertheless proved to be one of the major strengths of the expedition. They in turn were watched with equal interest, as they demonstrated the construction of a boat from the stripped bark of a forest tree, as they moved up and down the river on fishing trips, and as they whiled away the evenings with the bamboo and rattan puzzles which were to test the mental agility of many an expedition participant. They were always ready to help, whether with advice on roofing techniques or in arranging transport up river to the base camp.

To this camp came over 1,200 visitors. Each was required to become a member of MNS, and made a booking at the society's office, where the staff coped expertly (if not always phlegmatically) with the tremendous work load. Once a radio telephone had been borrowed it was quite a simple matter for Leong or Heah to liaise with the office staff — so long as the radio in Endau-Rompin was carried up the tree tower to improve

Far left: A comfortable bed and freedom from mosquitos make all the difference to camp life. (KBH)
Left: Base camp's most popular facility. (TYP)

Top: Sub-camps were all set near water, as at Padang Temambong. (HHH)
Above: A double decker camp design at Buaya Sangkut fitted more people into less space. (CSE)
Left: Activity at base camp continued well into the night. (TV3)

reception. Twice a week by prior arrangement, Leong and Heah would drive out one group, and collect the next group waiting at Kahang police station. This was no mean task, as the journey from Kahang to camp took over three hours: a hazardous two-hour trip by four-wheel drive vehicle along old logging tracks and across rickety log bridges, an hour's boat ride up the Sungai Endau, and a brisk walk in to camp.

On such trips the drivers would be armed with a formidable shopping list. With up to 50 visitors in camp at peak periods, all of them working up big appetites, the amount of fresh fish, meat, fruit and vegetables consumed was staggering. All this had to be purchased and tightly packed together with the new visitors and their belongings into the two vehicles for the return to camp.

For first-timers, this trip was itself an adventure. The ride was bumpy but exciting, the track lined by forest. Leopard, wild pigs, barking deer, binturong, turtles and snakes were some of the animals glimpsed along the

Left: Plenty of space in camp for working, eating and relaxing. **(GC)**
Below: The journey up river took anywhere from 30 minutes to 2 hours. **(GC)**

Far left: Some passengers preferred to walk when the vehicle crossed wooden bridges on the way to Endau-Rompin. **(TYP)**
Centre: Frequent rain ensured a slippery ride to Kampung Peta. **(TYP)**
Left: Changing river levels made the return trip easier for some than for others. Compare this with the same log bridge on page 185. **(GC)**

Top: The schools programme
included a quiz with a 'hands-on'
approach. (KR)
Above: Over 400 students were able
to visit the expedition. (TS)

way, in between dodging the pot-
holes and negotiating the bridges.

Visitors were of three main catego-
ries: scientists, students and volunteers. Whenever possible volunteers
were required to help the scientists in
their research, such as recording rainfall, and bringing back water samples
and bags of leaf litter. There were
always plenty of other tasks, like cut-
ting and maintaining trails, washing
dishes and repairing camp, preparing
meals, and guiding new groups into
the forest.

For education and research two
main walks were identified. One led
along the Jasin valley to Kuala Marong
and on to the Upeh Guling waterfall.
The other, a much tougher but shorter trip, climbed up the Janing ridge,
past the tree tower to the fan palm
forest and the curious hilltop swamp.
Early in the expedition signs were
placed along the Janing trail pointing
out curiosities like the walking-stick
palm and the pitcher plants, and more
basic features of the forest's functioning. From these signs developed the
nature trail with which all students
were introduced to the forest, its
trees, seedlings and fallen logs, fungi
and termites, so that they received a
general education in forest ecology.
Back in camp they might take part in
one of the research projects, like the
study of leeches. This particular project caused some apprehension at
first, followed by wild excitement.
Usually included in the younger students' itinerary was a contest to find
the smallest fruit, the biggest leaf,
and so on.

In this way MNS was able to involve some 400 schoolchildren directly in nature-related activities, while
university students received more
technical training from their accom-
panying teachers.

Most visits by pupils were concentrated in the school holidays, in
August and April, and at these times

Top, left: Tiger leeches **Haemadipsa picta** are more arboreal, and have a more painful bite than the commoner species. **(JD)**
Top: Providing blood for the leech study became a status symbol amongst schoolchildren. **(TYP)**
Above: Leech **Haemadipsa zeylanica,** sensitive to heat and vibration in seeking out a meal. **(JD)**

Far left: Briefings for students were an essential part of their introduction to the forest. **(KSN)**
Left: Catching prawns for measurement and release was a project in which everyone could help. **(KSN)**

Top: Looking for algae in the clear
water of Sungai Marong. (HHH)
Above: Measurements showed
Sungai Marong to have the purest
water of any river studied in the
country. (HHH)

Right: Sixty-six mosses were found
in Endau-Rompin. (KBH)
Facing page: Simple instruments
allowed a check on the direction of
ancient lava flows. (PG)

MNS received a great deal of help from the army. Their larger boats were able to accommodate more passengers, but did require more pushing through the shallows than the MNS rubber dinghy. A commando unit spent some time camping in the forest while working on the construction of the tree tower at the foot of Gunung Janing. Meanwhile the Air Force generously provided helicopters for making aerial surveys and transporting some of the bulkier equipment.

Work In Progress

With so many scientists working in the area, volunteers could usually find some interesting task to perform. Tiny aquatic animals and plants could be collected by sweeping fine nets through the water. For small mammal trapping, wire cage-traps had to be carried from place to place. Much more care and supervision were needed for some tasks than others. Collection of moths from a white sheet, lit at night by a powerful lamp, was a relatively simple task, and the scientists and their technical assistants were able to show many volunteers how to pin out the catch in the required manner for later study. Much of the geological work could be done on the spot, by simple examination of rock-types by lens and eye, but for others carefully labelled collections had to be taken back to the laboratory. There dissections, chemical analyses, or detailed microscopical examination might be necessary.

Observing and reporting on all these events, members of the press and television stations paid visits to the base camp. From this resulted a steady flow of articles, and later broadcasts, which ensured continuing public interest in the expedition. Only when the expedition was under way did it become clear how its component parts depended on one another.

Right: **Musa gracilis** *under study, the smallest Malaysian wild banana.* (DL)
Below, right: Use of electric probes permitted a thorough study of fish diversity. (HHH)
Below: Scientists and volunteers cooperate in preparing specimens. (KSN)
Bottom: Tracks radiated from base camp to study sites like Pulau Jasin and Gunung Janing. (MG)

Centre: Simple tools yield quick results in assessing moth abundance. (JD)
Left: Forest skills include thorough familiarity with map and compass. (TS)
Below: Old window blinds make clear, durable signs. (KR)
Bottom: A rope and a team spirit link expedition participants. (KSN)

Without public interest funds would not have been forthcoming. Without this, scientific work would have been impossible. Without the scientific projects to see and take part in, schoolchildrens' visits would have been of limited value, and the flow of information on progress and findings would have dried up. Further aspects of this relationship were provided by a group of artists, who came to capture Endau-Rompin's beauty with pencil and brush, and by the arrival of Datuk Shahrir bin Abdul Samad, then Federal Territory Minister.

That a government minister should take the time to see personally the expedition in progress was a great boost to morale. It demonstrated the impact of the expedition and the importance of Endau-Rompin; indeed, the expedition was making news not only in Malaysia but also internationally.

So the expedition went on, with only minor hitches such as a late arrival one day or a vehicle repair another. It was clear from an early stage that, with so much interest and so many visitors, the duration of the adventure would have to be extended beyond the six months of the original plan. In the end the Malaysian Heritage and Scientific Expedition ran for a full 13 months, from June 2 1985 to June 30 1986.

Knowing the force with which monsoon weather could strike the eastern side of the peninsula, the MNS was prepared for heavy rain and floods to cause a hiatus in operations towards the end of 1985. But November and December passed with only a little wet weather, and work continued without interruption. January and February continued hot and dry. Time was spent re-roofing the camp, improving the roads and repairing bridges. Then, as February drew to a close, it started to pour.

Top: Up or down? Careful control of the dinghy is needed to avoid an accident. **(HHH)**
Above: Even the television crew had to take the slow route to camp. **(A)**

Above: Floods leave a few problems behind; volunteers smooth them out. **(CSE)**

Far left: With ingenuity, even deep mud proves no obstacle. **(MS)**

Left: Given enough helping hands, most repairs were quick. **(TV3)**

Storms could cause sudden damage. **(MS)**

Coming Of The Monsoon

For the first two days the rain merely soaked the ground and nothing extraordinary was seen. But the rains became heavier and heavier. The winds became stronger, and soon a completely different atmosphere pervaded the landscape. The weather dominated everything.

The sun disappeared, and for about ten days it rained non-stop. At the camp, the rain gauge simply overflowed. Empty buckets left outdoors quickly filled to the brim. The wind rose to hurricane level. It swept through the valleys sending the moisture-laden trees crashing. It swiped through base camp like a giant boxing glove, raising the roof of the sleeping quarters and scattering thatch and timber in all directions. It demolished the generator shed and drove the rain into everything, even through the roof that managed to stay intact.

The rivers reacted with violence. At first they rose slowly, and by the fourth or fifth day they seemed to have stabilised. Then, as the entire valley became saturated, the rivers swelled and pulsed with each new rainstorm. The water level of Sungai Jasin rose at startling speed, flooding the log bridge which gave access and exit to base camp. All the shingle beaches disappeared and the piles of driftwood near the camp were swept away. The log bridge began to shift

downstream until the cable became taut as for a high wire act. When the flood finally subsided, the bridge's end settled some eight feet further downstream.

As the Sungai Endau rose and overflowed its banks, it brought floods to new areas with each rise in the water level. The debris carried down with the powerful current made it almost impossible to travel upstream, even with a 15 horsepower motor on the rubber dinghy. Then, as the lower valley filled up, the storm peaked.

When the river reached its maximum height of some five metres, the large clump of bamboo high on the bank at Kampung Peta was standing in water. The Orang Hulu said they would have evacuated had the water level risen another two metres. Some families had started to pack.

The expedition boathouse at Kuala Jasin stood in two feet of water. As the rapids, waterfalls and islands disappeared under water, getting to base camp became a simple matter of boating up the Endau, turning left and landing practically at the camp doorstep. Previously, it had been necessary to walk the last 500 metres to the camp, after a one-hour ride often punctuated with stops to push the boat through shallow waters.

Then just as suddenly the water level dropped, 3.6 metres in a single day. And instead of riding smoothly over the rapids right to base camp, one had to negotiate the dinghy carefully over the falls.

Naturally, such terrible weather left a trail of destruction. Where the expedition was concerned, it left many participants stranded when the floods cut off roads and washed away the bridges. But, more important, all who witnessed the fury of the monsoon were left with a profound respect for the power of nature.

Far left: In March, the monsoon comes at last. **(MS)**
Left: Gentle falls become angry torrents after rain. **(MS)**

Above: Floods necessitate a new method of entry to base camp. **(MS)**
Left: The peak of the flood: suddenly boats can reach the doorstep. **(MS)**

orang hulu

The people of the Endau-Rompin area belong to the group usually called Orang Jakun, but also referred to sometimes by the general names Orang Asli or Orang Hulu. They have traditionally been collectors of forest produce such as resins, rattan and camphor-wood. From time to time their settlements have shifted: this has allowed the recovery of the forest in one place as another was exploited, a good example of man living in harmony with nature — conservation at work. Evidence of older settlements up-river can still be seen in places, where a few coconut trees or a cultivated mango survive on the river bank.

Much of their life has depended and still depends on the rivers. Fish is an important food item, and the men spend a lot of time fishing. They use ordinary narrow boats made from planking, but they also make dug-outs from a single piece of wood. Dug-outs have a very shallow draught, and the boatman must balance carefully when using the pole or paddle. Very light canoes are made from bark sheets stripped from a tree. A bark canoe was seen on the Sungai Endau by anthropologist Ivor Evans in 1915, and villagers made one at Kampung Peta during the expedition.

In recent years the Orang Hulu have become more settled and live in in permanent villages. Their children have started to go to government schools. Kampung Peta, the village closest to the expedition base camp, is accessible only by means of a run-down old logging track two hour's drive from the nearest tarmac road, or by river.

The Orang Hulu, then, are fairly remote from the outside world. But as traders of produce they have had plenty of contact with others. Even as early as 1892, when H.W. Lake journeyed up the Endau and met them, he reported that elements of aboriginal language were already disappearing. In the stories told by the expedition guides and boatmen, however, a part of the Orang Hulu culture is preserved. The many references in their stories to the forest, rocks, and especially the rivers of Endau-Rompin go to show how close is the link between the Orang Hulu and the natural world about them.

Below: Kampung Peta, home of the Orang Hulu. (LYK)

Left: Fruit trees shade the village meeting-place. (JD)
Below, left: Earth retains heat for slow thorough cooking. (KBH)
Below: A temporary camp of palm leaves can be made in minutes. (KSN)

Above: Visitors to Kampung Peta raise plenty of curiosity. (MG)
Left: Building of bark canoes, an ancient craft, is now confined to Sungai Endau. (TS)

folklore

THE CURSE OF THE EAGLE

Long ago, in the days of our great-great grandfathers, there lived in the Endau valley a giant by the name of Datuk Sang Kelamai. He was not only large but also wise and peace-loving. He married a strong maiden from Gunung Tahan and lived a contented life hunting and fishing along the Sungai Endau.

One day a huge eagle descended from the sky to live among the men in the valley. The eagle would perch on a tall tree and swoop down to catch and carry away whosoever's name had been called out loud.

Before long the people in the valley and the neighbouring countryside were losing their wives, husbands and children as the eagle eagerly picked them up when their name was called by their loved ones. So the villagers and the people of the valley started to talk in whispers and lamented the loss of their loved ones carried away and never seen again.

Thus the eagle became the curse of the village and everyone put their heads together to solve the problem of removing the dreadful curse afflicting them. A few foolhardy youths had tried and were killed by one swift sudden attack by the eagle. And no one had magic powerful enough to vanquish it.

Everyone was sad and at their wits' end. The problem was brought to Datuk Sang Kelamai who thought of a simple plan relying on the eagle's readiness to catch and carry off whatever or whoever was called aloud by name.

Watched by the whole village, Datuk Sang Kelamai stood by the river. He pointed to a huge rock by the Sungai Endau and called its name out loud, "Batu Penunggul!" (fixed rock). The eagle responded at once to the call and swooped swiftly down and grasped the rock in its talons to carry it off. But however much he flapped his mighty wings, the eagle could not lift the rock. After several days the rock still held fast and the struggles of the mighty eagle weakened until he died of exhaustion.

The villagers and all the people of the Endau valley were thus rid of the curse of the eagle, and thanks to the wisdom of Datuk Sang Kelamai life returned to normal and the people lived once more in peace. To this day Batu Penunggul stands by the Sungai Endau above Kampung Peta and is an important landmark of the river.

THE OLD MAN OF ENDAU

Peaceful days did not last forever. It was not long after the eagle was vanquished that news reached the Endau valley that the Bugis from an island south of Johor were at war with the people of the coast. Reports of wars where hundreds and thousands of people were killed brought anxiety and concern to the hearts of the peaceful people of the Endau valley.

Everyone in the valley was jittery and watchful for any sign of possible attack. However, although they waited apprehensively, no Bugis ever came to attack the valley.

The giant, Datuk Sang Kelamai and his wife went out fishing and hunting one day. It was a successful day. Datuk Sang Kelamai had speared an elephant, which he cut into pieces and placed in his boat. He had also caught some Kelesa fish and had scaled and cleaned them ready for dinner. In the process of scaling the fish, two large fish scales lodged in his eyes impairing his vision.

As they rowed home upriver, the coconut shell used for bailing knocked about in the bottom of the boat with the rocking motion of rowing. In the quiet of the evening, Datuk Sang Kelamai thought he heard the war drums of the Bugis approaching. Through the fish scales he had the impression that the water in the distance was churned up by thousands of rowing boats.

In alarm, Datuk Sang Kelamai shouted to his wife to row upriver for their lives. His wife seeing nothing and not being alarmed by the knocking of the empty coconut shell did not understand what Datuk Sang Kelamai's excitement was all about. In the confusion, Datuk Sang Kelamai rowed with all his might while his wife used all her strength to keep the boat where it was. As a result the boat broke into two.

Datuk Sang Kelamai in his half of the boat shot upriver scattering the pieces of elephant along the way. The elephant's head forms the rock that can be seen along the river between Kampung Peta and Kampung Punan. The midsection of the elephant can be seen at Kuala Kenu up the Sungai Endau.

In his flight, Datuk Sang Kelamai rowed right up to the source of the Endau and hid himself as a rock at the bottom of the cliff. Today if you travel up to the source of the Endau at the foot of Gunung Besar, you can see Datuk Sang Kelamai in the form of a huge rock. There the water of the Sungai Endau enters his mouth and leaves below the base of the rock. The waters of the Sungai Endau are thus considered the gift of Datuk Sang Kelamai, who is also known as the Old Man Of the Endau.

THE DRONGO – THE KING OF BIRDS

In the days when birds could talk, the birds of the world decided that they should have a king to rule over them and maintain an orderly society.

The Rhinoceros Hornbill was chosen and given the crown. However, he flew about proclaiming his new status so loudly that soon all the birds regretted their decision. But they were unable to retrieve the crown, so to this day the Rhinoceros Hornbill still flies around the forest with this red and yellow crown and he still calls as loudly as ever.

Next the eagle was made king because of his majesty and poise. However, much to the dismay of all the smaller birds, their new king had an insatiable appetite for them and killed and ate his own subjects.

The cruel regime of the eagle was eventually overthrown by a rebellion led by the Drongo who chased the eagle away. In the eagle's place, the Drongo was proclaimed King of Birds and he chose the Spider Hunter for his prime minister to help him rule his subjects, which they continue to do to this day.

Indeed, it is not unusual in the forest to see an eagle being chased by a pair of drongos. The chirping of the Spider Hunter flying about in the forest is considered by the Orang Hulu as the prime minister going about his business of running the bird world.

SERJARANG GIGI – THE HAIRY GIANT

From ancient times, the Endau valley has been inhabited by a tribe of hairy giants with huge widely spaced teeth (Serjarang Gigi). These hairy giants have arms the size of a man's leg and are well over eight feet tall. They can appear and disappear at will and are very skillful and knowledgeable in forest craft. They are also great linguists and can speak any language spoken to them. They have also the ability to tell your name even if they have never met you before. Nowadays they seem to be rare.

The Serjarang Gigi giants used to catch individuals wandering in the forest and eat them near streams or rivers. When they met a wanderer, they would demand that he address them by their right name. If he failed, the wanderer would be eaten.

One day, a Serjarang Gigi giant came across a man alone in the forest and demanded whether he knew the giant's name. When the man could not answer, he picked the poor fellow up and carried him under his arm over hill and dale to the banks of the river to feast on him. The man kept cool and planned his escape. Seeing the giant's hairy body he reached for his "*gobek api" and set the hair on fire. The giant was set ablaze and dropped the man, who made his escape. From that day on the Serjarang Gigi giants learned to respect man and to dread fire of any kind, and have given up the habit of eating people.

* fire-making tools comprising a pestle and cylinder

from the log book

"30 September, p.m. Two exhausted wild men crawled out of the jungle, half-dead, clothes in tatters, soaked to the skin: Jimmy and Shah. They walked in from Kampung Selai, 5 days."

"Went out in the evening to block off the notorious hornet nest near Kuala Marong. These vicious little monsters caused grief on several occasions. I managed to collect a few stings from them, as well as a specimen for science."

"So I proceeded, lit by starlight and by luminescent logs glowing eerily along beneath the river. At Kuala Bong the water became too deep to wade. I crawled along semi-submerged logs for a while, then was forced to scramble up the cliff into the jungle. To my amazement the forest was glowing with a carpet of luminescent fungi, making it possible for me to make my way. I halted by a stationary spot of blue light suspended in mid-air — a glow worm sitting on a leaf."

Dan Walker Sept. 1985

"For us students , the expedition has taught us many things. We explored the jungle and all its phases. We're glad to come here. The students never thought of having this kind of jungle here. All we had in mind was thick jungle with snakes and thick undergrowth, not high trees with very little undergrowth beneath it."

Cikgu Zaid and his 7 students, MRSM, Kulim, Kedah. 18/10/85

"Salleh from the IMR team saw a wild boar's head at the Sungai Jasin waterfall. It was not there the day before, presumably having been left there by a "kucing" the night before. Atan had actually seen a tiger at the camp entrance when he and Yeap were the only people staying there."

Gerard Cheong 5/7/85

"Endau-Rompin, probably one of the most beautiful places I have ever been. Some of the things I saw here, I had never seen before. There is no other journey like the journey to Endau-Rompin, nor maybe another base camp like the one at Endau-Rompin."

Faisal de Silva, age 9, 15/8/85

"This documentary is for you, and we hope we can show and tell all about Endau-Rompin the way you would like it to be told. We are proud to do such a documentary, not only because of what the expedition has achieved and the heritage value of Endau-Rompin, but also because it is a challenge to make a natural history documentary. Something Malaysian television has not ventured into, till now."

Nina Halim Rasip (TV3) June 1986

Saya akan cuba mempertahankan keaslian hutan rimba di Malaysia ini dari terokai oleh pengusaha-pengusaha pembalakan.

Hishamuddin Ahmad 9/8/85

"Richard found two small red crabs in the Monkey Cups on the ridge (actually Azmi found the first one). These were collected and brought back to base camp where they were the subject of a detailed close-up photo session and a long-drawn argument on whether the crab fell into the monkey cup or had chosen to live there happily of its own accord."

Tarlochan Singh, July 1985

"The kitchen caught fire at the pressure-lamp storage area. Quick action by all in camp — journalists, workers, Leong, Zaman (slight burn on his legs) and others — using all the water in camp managed to put out the fire within minutes."

Heah Hock Heng 8/8/85

"Then we heard, quite unmistakably and quite close, a low deep growl, reasonably menacing! Unable to believe it we waited, and heard it a second time! We decided to move back to camp fast, and heard the growl two or three times. No doubt about it — it was a big cat telling us to go home or else!"

Ilsa Sharp, October 1985

"Pauline had 53 leeches on her legs. It was some catch!"

Richard Lim, June 17 1985

"Chopper arrived in a.m., hovered briefly, dropped a note explaining that it would return in the afternoon, and flew off. Predictably we didn't see the note, and spent 6 hours in the blue funk which descends upon people who think they have been abandoned to die in the forest."

Danny Walker Sept. 1985

Yah! About the food. Wow! Bombastic!

Chia Kok Fan 6/8/85

Ekspedisi ini telah memberi banyak pengalaman, pengajaran yang banyak kepada saya.

Hashim Basir

"Last night one of the students asked me why it took the Government so long after 1940 to establish the second National Park. It wasn't an easy question, but the fact one of the students asked the question was a demonstration of the impact of the expedition on their thinking."

Datuk Shahrir bin Abdul Samad, Federal Territory Minister, August 1985

"Dennis caught an enormous stick insect from the ferns near camp. It is yellow, six inches long, and looks like an old leaf. It also bites."

Ruth Kiew, 11 June 1985

"As we climbed down the Sungai Jala Berani, I dislodged a cobble which ricocheted 200 feet down the slope and bounced off Idris's back-pack, a circumstance which he found highly amusing."

Danny Walker Sept. 1985

"A couple more days' stay would have moved the children more into the swing of camping life, although camp is so well organised that it really isn't camping as I know it. With a restaurant, 5 meals a day, flush toilets, running water basin and ready beds, it's more like a holiday motel!"

Mrs. Annie Cheah Sept. 1985

This is the most wonderful stay I have experienced and I wish I didn't have to leave.

Tan Bee Lin 31/7/85

Endau-Rompin is ......
- Cruising up to camp in the S.S. Bloody Hell
- Asking the Camp Manager to ring your wife/husband/ mother to say that you're not ready to come home
- hating people who come in by helicopter
- waking up to the melody of birds in the morning
- much, much, much better than Club Med
- languid afternoons in the jaccuzzis by the waterfall
- convincing others that staying in camp all day is not lounging around
- puffing up the Janing/Sengongong trail
- getting high on ethyl acetate at the moth trap
- wondering when the Endau-Rompin Bank is going to introduce ETC booths
- making bad, bad puns (get it, get it)
- conning new arrivals to do the washing up
- making life miserable for the camp manager
- skinny dipping at night
- having to survive the hardship of jungle fare like:

  Banana and apple crumble
  Hainanese Chicken rice
  Sambal Tumis Petai
  7 flavours of ice cream
  Ice cold beer
  Endauberry pancakes
  Curry puffs
  Chicken curry mee
  Chapatti with dhall

- Having army rations "for a change"
- Trying to drown out the snoring of your neighbour by snoring even louder
- Losing half the camp's supply of dining utensils while washing up
- Trying to write something intelligent in the log book!

– En-daufinitions –
by Yang Chong and Rohani Jelani

Our sincere thanks to all who gave us more than we can return.

Dilys Yap 27/8/85

Hope the beautiful places will be here for some time to come. I'll like to bring my great-grandkids here and show them where I had one of the best experience of my life.

Azleena Salleh 9/8/85

May the jungle live forever.

Khong Weng Tuck 31/7/85

the
WAY AHEAD

the way ahead

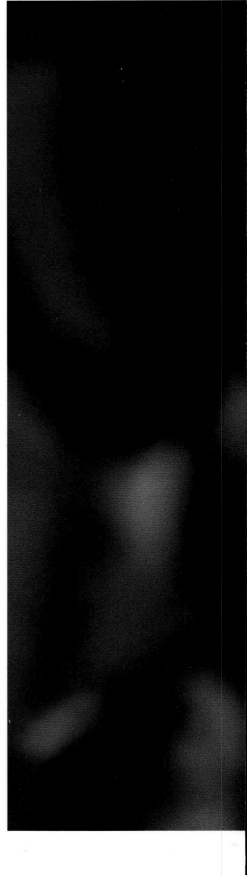

The flag was finally lowered on June 30th 1986 to mark the close of the expedition. The Endau-Rompin expedition had run a year. It had been a year Malaysians will not easily forget, especially with the continuous flow of reports in the mass media about the scientific discoveries being made and the lovely natural landscapes found in the area. The exciting happenings and rewarding activities experienced by all those scientists, volunteers, and students participating in the expedition were also very well reported.

With this constant flow of information, Endau-Rompin was sustained as a very current topic. The man-in-the-street knew where Endau-Rompin was and what was happening there. Never before in the history of this country had any conservation issue enjoyed such sustained public support and interest.

For all those who had been touched by the aura and charm of Endau-Rompin, the closing of the expedition must have been received with mixed feelings - sad that it had to end so soon and glad that it was indeed a great success. Nevertheless, they all nursed and shared that very strong hope that, somehow, those in a position to provide the protection needed for Endau-Rompin would now be moved to take bold and firm steps forward, to conserve its natural beauty and resources.

Realities

Many have asked why Endau-Rompin was identified as a critical area for conservation and was being targetted by the Federal Government of Malaysia as a national park. Before

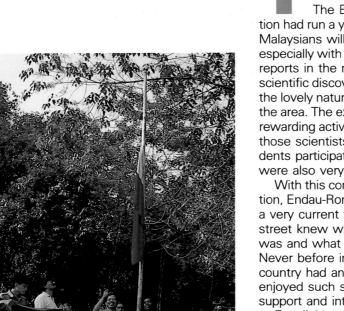

Above: The way ahead. **(TS)**

Previous page:
Main: Dawn steals gently over the forest. **(KR)**
Inset, left: Hemipteran nymph, a feeder on plant sap.
Inset, right: Pig-tailed macaques **Macaca nemestrina** *move through the forest in big troupes.* **(*AJ)**

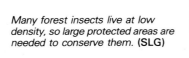

Many forest insects live at low density, so large protected areas are needed to conserve them. **(SLG)**

the expedition, the reasons for the choice were still being challenged. However, the wealth of information generated from the expedition, as is evident from the preceding pages, all points to the strategic importance of the area in maintaining environmental and ecological stability. These include:

- **The area serves as an important catchment for the main rivers of Endau and Rompin** which implies that damage to this forest would result in undesirable effects downstream, such as flooding, rapid fluctuations of water levels, and increased sediment load which is harmful to the fish resource in the river itself and in the coastal region.

- **The area is generally hilly with many valleys drained by numerous small streams.** This implies that exploitation of the area would be costly not only in terms of investment capital but also in terms of damage to the environment, particularly soil erosion.

- **Many different and some unique ecological habitats have now been found within a day's walk of each other,** each with its own characteristic set of plant species. To locate another similar area in Peninsular Malaysia with so many eco-habitats within a short distance of each other would be extremely difficult. This enhances the value of the area not only for conservation of biological resources but also for tropical forest research, education, and recreation.

Natural pop-art: **Dipteris lobbiana** *around the roots of* **Tristania whiteana.** (KR)

- **Many new species of plants and animals have been discovered and recorded during the expedition.** Our scientists have located many plant species that are absolutely unique to this area. It is reported that there are still many more to be discovered. Should this area be damaged and exploited it is highly probable that this endemic flora and fauna will be destroyed, and lost to Malaysians for ever.

- **There is a rich diversity of wild orchids in Endau-Rompin,** largely because of the numerous eco-habitats represented. This area therefore could serve as an important natural repository from which genetic material could be obtained to develop orchid hybrids, following scientific research and documentation. There are many unique forest types in the area that still need further scientific studies. This is especially the case with respect to nutrient poor habitats, where research could provide many insights into current concepts of management of denuded lands.

- **The area is rich in wildlife with many of the important and rare species known to be resident in the forests here.** This represents the most important refuge in the whole country for the Sumatran rhinoceros, a species that is fast becoming extinct. Some members of the expedition saw evidence of their presence in the area.

- Although parts of the Sungai Endau showed evidence of the effects of past logging, a heavy silt load, **many of the other river systems were still in their pristine**

The rarity or abundance of reptiles is hard to assess, as they are seldom encountered. Spiny hill tortoise **Heosemys spinosa.** (SLG)

condition. This makes the area amenable to recreational activities.

- The area once properly managed will have **great potential for developing educational and recreational facilities** which could in turn serve to enhance tourism in the country.

What Next For Endau-Rompin?

Malaysia is already fast losing its natural forest cover. In Peninsular Malaysia there is only one area which is guaranteed some form of protection, this being the national park Taman Negara. This was declared in 1939. Since then, we have yet to gazette another. Why is this so? It cannot be that Malaysians are ignorant of the reasons for setting aside natural forest strictly for conservation, to protect our rich and varied biological resources, so as to maintain a gene pool for future endeavours.

The conservation of Endau-Rompin has been an issue ever since its identification under the Third Malaysia Plan of 1976. At that time the area designated for protection was 200,000 hectares. Yet over the years this has been whittled down to a mere 87,000 hectares as given in the Fifth Malaysia Plan of 1986. What happened will remain a mystery to many. What is now worrying is that, while the Park status remains unsettled, time is slipping by. The immediate implementation of steps for management of the area is of utmost urgency as it is now known that logging has taken place in the very heart of the proposed Endau-Rompin Park.

It is therefore very heartening to note that the two State Governments have finally come out in unison with

Left: The forest helps protect natural features like waterfalls. **(WKM)**
Right: Diversity of habitats, like the orchid-laden Pulau Jasin, gives Endau-Rompin special value. **(KR)**

statements to designate Endau-Rompin as an area for conservation. Furthermore, they expect to gazette the areas under separate State Park Acts, which will be drawn up with all the clauses of the National Parks Act incorporated. This strategy being adopted by the states is a welcome sign that they are now convinced that the area should be managed and conserved as a wilderness park.

Yet, this is not sufficient for the future of Endau-Rompin. What is needed is a proper management plan for the area which sets out the long term policies for the protection and conservation of designated resources. Otherwise, with unplanned and *ad hoc* decisions being taken, the chances are slim that the area will be conserved effectively.

As Malaysians we should realise that Endau-Rompin is very much our own natural heritage and one that is in fact held in trust for us by the State Governments of Johor and Pahang. Ultimately, it is still the responsibility of each and every Malaysian citizen to see to it that the trustees manage Endau-Rompin in a manner that does not jeopardise its ultimate function as the habitat for the few remaining natural forest types in south Malaysia, within which many unique examples of our flora and fauna can be found.

Increasing World-wide Awareness For Rain Forest Conservation

There is today unprecedented worldwide concern over the fate of tropical forests, especially since they are disappearing at the rate of 11 million hectares per year. This concern stems from the gradual realisation over the last 15 years or so of the

Clean river water depends on undisturbed forest catchments. (YPK)

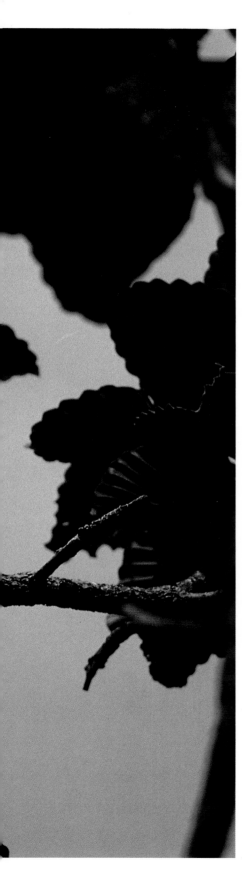

immense strategic role that such ecosystems play in maintaining global environmental quality and stability. There are already numerous studies and reports demonstrating that many ecological upheavals in the tropical environment can be linked to excessive and intensive deforestation. Detectable changes in local weather patterns, in water quality, and in nutrient status of the soils are invariably the result.

Recent studies have also highlighted the immense diversity of biological resources that are to be found within such tropical forest ecosystems. The high plant and animal diversity so characteristic of tropical forests is largely attributable to stability over evolutionary time, which has allowed for the accretion of species through adaptive strategies to exploit the environment. It is now estimated that almost half of all known animal and plant species in the world today are to be found in tropical rain forests.

Many of these resources have economic potential. Yet in most developing countries where tropical forests abound, the local socio-economic and political environments have unfortunately favoured the relentless exploitation of the natural forests, primarily for timber. With the export of such tropical hardwoods to developed countries, valuable foreign exchange has been easily generated (with little capital investment and effort) to sustain their national development. In so doing, vast acreages of forest land have been damaged and devastated, some to the extent that it will take another two life-

times before they can even recover. Some never will. As a result, many economic opportunities have been lost simply because the forests have not been exploited for their real worth. Coupled to this, many environmental problems are created that will need much financial input to rectify. However, this state of affairs need not necessarily prevail. Incorporating proper utilisation of the forests with efforts made to conserve the resources today, will make its impact tomorrow.

To many politicians and policy-makers in the government, the word conservation often gets linked with a "don't touch" approach that they believe is advocated by environmentalists. This is a fallacy. Conservation of a resource in very simple terms means its proper management so that it can be sustained over future time. Management of our forest resources necessarily means that some areas will have to be exploited. Yet, like a wise banker who will always maintain some reserve funds, some critical forest areas should be set aside unexploited, and managed along different lines, for future economic potential that has yet to be realised. It is also necessary to leave behind some pristine forest areas for generations that follow us.

Endau-Rompin has now been identified as one such area. The state governments of Johor and Pahang will need to formulate carefully their management plans with the objective of enforcing strict conservation of natural resources in the area and of protecting their watersheds.

Scarlet minivet **Pericrocotus flammeus.** *Plants, water, land and animals are linked in mutual dependence.* **(MS)**

(MS)

APPENDICES

credits

BOOK COMMITTEE

Dr. G.W.H. Davison
Ms. Kok Swee Ngor
Ms. Lee Su Win
Ms. Low Eng Sim
Mr. Tarlochan Singh
Ms. Wee, Margaret

Editor
G.W.H. Davison

TEXT CREDITS

G.W.H. Davison
Heah Hock Heng
Kiew Bong Heang
Kiew, Ruth
Lai Food See
Lee Su Win
Lim Meng Tsai
Lim, Richard P.
Monk, Kathryn Ann
Phang Siew Moi
Saw Leng Guan
Shaharin Yussof
Sharp, Ilsa
Tarlochan Singh
Taylor, Charlotte
Tho Yow Pong
Tunku Mohd Nazim Yaacob
Walker, Daniel
Wong Khoon Meng
Yap Son Kheong

PHOTO CREDITS

A	Anonymous
AJ	Allen Jeyarajasingam
A/ME	Alan & Madeleine Ernst
CSE	Chin Sock Ee
CT	Charlotte Taylor
DL	Dirk Limann
DW	Daniel Walker
FSPN	Francis S P Ng
GC	Gerald Cubitt
	Natural History Photographer
GD	Geoffrey Davison
HHH	Heah Hock Heng
HM	Haji Mohamad
IM	Idris Mohamad
JD	John Dawn
KBH	Kiew Bong Heang
KM	Kathryn Monk
KR	Ken Rubeli
	Natural History Photographer
KSN	Kok Swee Ngor
LC	Lena Chan
LFS	Lai Food See
LYK	Leong Yueh Kwong
MG	Marlane Guelden
MK	Michael Kavanagh
MS	Morten Strange
	Bird Photographer (Flying Colours)
PG	Peter Gathercole
	Natural History Photographer
PSM	Phang Siew Moi
RA	Rahimatsah Amat
RBS	Robert B. Steubing
SLG	Saw Leng Guan
SY	Shaharin Yussof
TJH	Tan Jiew Hoe
TMNY	Tunku Mohd Nazim Yaacob
TS	Tarlochan Singh
TV3	TV3
TYP	Tho Yow Pong
WKM	Wong Khoon Meng
WYS	Wong Young Soon
YPK	Yap Piang Kian
*	taken in captivity

Special thanks are due to the following for their assistance in identification of photographs

Dr M.A. Haji Mohamed
Dr Kiew Bong Heang
Dr Ruth Kiew
Dr J. Kuthubudeen
Saw Leng Guan
Dr Tho Yow Pong
Wong Khoon Meng

Illustrations of Folklore by courtesy of Teh Yew Kiang

Design Layout And Production
Kok Swee Ngor

Typesetting
Cytron (M) Sdn. Bhd.

Colour Separation
Far East Offset and Engraving Sdn. Bhd.

Printing
Print & Co. Sdn. Bhd.

Photo of YTM Tunku Abdul Rahman Putra Al-Haj by courtesy of Teh Pek Leng (Malayan Tung Bao Daily News).

major donors
to the Malaysian Heritage and Scientific Expedition, Endau-Rompin, 1985/86

Ace Canning Corp. Sdn. Berhad
American Express (M) Sdn. Berhad
Aminah Syed Mohamed
Anthonian Distributors Sdn. Berhad
Arab Malaysian Bank
Atlas Ice Sdn. Berhad
Ayer Molek Rubber Co. Berhad
Ban Seng Properties Sdn. Berhad
Bandaraya Developments Sdn. Berhad
Briggs, JGR
Bukit Katil Rubber Estate Berhad
CUSO
Carlsberg Brewery (M) Berhad
Central Province Wellesley Transport Co.
  Sdn. Berhad
Chan Hong Ee
Chang Yii Tan
Chong Chow Yang
Choo S. H.
Chye Clinic, Kepong Bahru
Ciba-Geigy (Malaysia) Sdn. Berhad
Citibank N.A.
Cobb, Timothy
Colgate-Palmolive (M) Sdn. Berhad
Dancall Sdn. Berhad
Diethelm Malaysia Sdn. Berhad
Drug Houses of Australia
Equatron (M) Sdn. Berhad
Federal Flour Mills
Federal Iron Works Sdn. Berhad
Federal Publications Sdn. Berhad
Foo, Michael
Foo, Rosalind
GCB Trading Sdn. Berhad
Gianfranco Ferre Boutique
Goethe Institute Staff & students
Goh Seng Aun
Guinness Malaysia Berhad
Guppy Plastics Industries Sdn. Berhad
Harrisons Malaysian Plantations Berhad
Hillcrest Gardens Sdn. Berhad
Interdesign Berakan
Ishihara Construction (M) Sdn. Berhad
Jaya Housing Corp. Sdn. Berhad
Jaya Shankar
Jebcon Sdn. Berhad
Klang Development Sdn. Berhad
Knowland, W.
Kumpulan Syed Kechik Sdn. Berhad
Kuok Brothers
Kuok Foundation
Lam Soon Oil & Soap Manufacturing
  Sdn. Berhad
Land Rover (M) Sdn. Berhad
Lee Heng Tiong
Lee Man Construction Co. Sdn. Bhd.
Leong Shown Chong
Lim Kee Jin

Lions Club, KL West
Lions Club, Subang Jaya
Longman Malaysia Sdn. Berhad
Malayan Nature Society, Johor Branch
Malayan Nature Society, Penang Branch
Malayan Nature Society, Selangor Branch
Malaysia Mining Corp Berhad
Malaysian Airlines System
Malaysian Resources Corp. Berhad
Malaysian Society for Marine Sciences, Penang
Malaysian Tobacco Company Berhad
Maran Road Sawmill Sdn. Berhad
May & Baker Sdn. Berhad
Meh Fatt Leong
Messrs Yeow & Chin, Johor
Metal Box (M) Berhad
Mountaineering Association Malaysia
Murni Properties Sdn. Berhad
National Art Gallery
Negara Properties Sdn. Berhad
Neoh Soon Kean
Ogilvy & Mather Public Relations Staff
Ong Lam Kiat
Paramount Malaysia Co. Sdn. Berhad
Penang O'Hara Floral Arts Society
Perak Turf Club
Perlis Plantations
Persatuan Pemborong-pemborong Beras
  Semenanjung Malaysia
Petaling Garden Berhad
Petroliam Nasional Berhad
Phillips, Richard
Rajakumar, M.J.
Redang Campers
Rotary Club, Bayan Baru, Penang
Rotary Club, Damansara
Rotary Club, Gombak
Rotary Club, Klang
Rotary Club, Petaling Jaya
Rotary Club, Pudu
Rurban Properties Sdn. Berhad
SMJK Chung Hwa Wei Sin, Terengganu
SMJK Chung Hwa, Kota Baru
SMJK Laki-laki Bukit Bintang
SMJK Perempuan Jalan Ampang
SMJK St. Andrew, Muar
Salma Ismail
Sawira Sdn. Berhad
Schoenburg, P.J.
Seah Kwang Hon
Selaman Sdn. Berhad
Selangor Pewter Co. Sdn. Berhad
Shah Alam Properties
Sharp, Ilsa
Smith & Nephew Sales Sdn. Berhad
Smith, B.A.R.
South Malaysia Industries Berhad
Sri Hartamas Development Sdn. Berhad

St. Mary's Secondary School
Star Publications (Malaysia) Berhad
Star Publications (Malaysia) Berhad,
  Penang (staff)
Star Reporters & Pixmen
Supreme Housing Developments Sdn. Berhad
Syarikat Desa Permai Sdn. Berhad
Syarikat Pertama Sdn. Berhad
TTDI-SEA Park Development Sdn. Berhad
Tan & Tan Development Sdn. Berhad
Tan Ah Tee
Tan Chong & son's Motor Co. Sdn. Berhad
Tan Jiew Hoe
Tan, Anthony
Tengku Maimunah Abu Bakar &
  Ungku Fatimah
Tiang Guan Rubber Estates
Tunku Maimunah Yaacob
Tunku Yaacob
UMW/Toyota-Sejati Motors
Ulu Yam Temple
United Italian Trading Co.
Utusan Melayu (M) Berhad
Wan Ibrahim Wan Hassan
Warrick (M) Sdn. Berhad
Wee Tiong Soon
Wellcome Malaysia Sdn. Berhad
Willoughby, John and family
Wong Andrew, Tracy and Tricia
Wong Chee Cheong
World Wildlife Fund Malaysia

Special thanks are due to **Star Publications (Malaysia) Berhad** and their staff for invaluable help throughout the expedition.

MNS would also like to thank the many donors who contributed small amounts which helped in the success of the expedition.

participants

ORGANISING COMMITTEE

Mr. Barlow, H.S.
Dr. Davison, G.W.H.
Dr. Kiew Bong Heang
  (Expedition Leader)
Mr. Koh Beng Huat
Ms. Lee Su Win
Dr. Lim, Richard P.
Dr. Salleh Mohd. Nor
Ms. Tan Bee Hwa
Mr. Tarlochan Singh
Mr. Yin Ee Kok
Mr. Yong Ghong Chong, Dennis

SCIENTIFIC COMMITTEE

Dr. Davison, G.W.H.
Dr. Kiew Bong Heang
Dr. Lim, Richard, P.
Dr. Ng, F.S.P.
Mr. Tarlochan Singh
Dr. Tho Yow Pong

Camp Managers

1) Mr. Yeap Soon Pin (June 1985)
2) Mr. Chin Shin Mun (July 1985)
3) Mr. Yong Ghong Chong, Dennis
   (June-July 1985)
4) Mr. Tang Fook Leong
   August 1985-June 1986)

Education Officer

Mr. Heah Hock Heng
(January-June 1986)

SCIENTISTS

Abdul Aziz Ahmad Shah
Andrews, Susyn
Avadhani, P.N.
Bradley, Peter
Chan Hon Fong
Charles, J.K.
Che Ghani Mohammad
Corlett, Richard
Davison, G.W.H.
Dekkers, Angustinus Josephus
Dransfield, John
Edwards, Peter J.
Fong Foo Woon
Goh Chong Jin

Goh, Hedy
Green, Paul
Haji Mohamed, M.A.
Ho Tze Ming
Idris Mohamad
Inder Singh
Jamaluddin Basharuddin
Kam Suan Pheng
Khashiyah Mohd. Hashim
Khelikuzzaman M Hussain
Khoo Teng Tiong
Kiew Bong Heang
Kiew, Ruth
Kirton, Colin
Kirton, Lawrence
Kochummen, K.M.
Lai Food See
Lee Chai Peng
Lee Khim Meng
Leong Yueh Kwong
Lim Meng Tsai
Lim Weng Hee
Lim, Richard P.
Louis, Isabelle
M. Sham M. Sani
Maryati Mohamed
Mohd. Samsudin Osman
Mohd. Zakaria Ismail
Monk, Kathryn Anne
Ng Sook Ming
Ng, S.P. Francis
Ooi, A.C. Peter
Phang Siew Moi
Rao, Anishesarppe Narayan
Salleh Mohd. Nor
Salma Idris
Sasekumar, A.
Saw Leng Guan
Scott, Eileen
Sedgwick, Walter
Sepiah Muid
Soepadmo, E.
Stuebing, Robert
Tan Chai Lin
Tan Teck Koon
Tan Tiong Wah, Hugh
Tarlochan Singh
Taylor, Charlotte E.
Tho Yow Pong
Wang, Florence
Wee Yeow Chin
Weiner, Jacob
Weir, John
Wells, David
Wong Khoon Meng
Yap Son Kheong
Zakaria Mohd. Kassim
Zubaid Akbar

VOLUNTEERS

Abdul Ghani Hashim
Abdul Karim Russ Hassan
Abdul Malek Sohot
Abdul Wahab Umar
Abdullah Piee
Abdullah Subir
Ahmad Farid Jamaluddin
Ahmad Tajudin Hj Hamid
Aini Omar
Alphonsa Arputham
Amar Singh
Aminah Babjan
Amutha Balan
Ang Ah Lian
Ang Chin Heng
Angan
Annez Faizal Ibrahim Bajunid
Audrey Catherine Shanta
Awtar Kaur
Ayau
Ayers, Edward
Azharuddin Zainal Abidin
Azizun Rahman
Azlina Salleh
Azmeer Salleh
Azmi Mayuddin
Baharuddin Bujang
Barkell, Martha
Barkell, William H.
Barlow, Henry
Baya Busu
Berg, Karin
Berger, Rachel
Bistaman Siru Abdul Rahman
Brockman, Alan Howard
Bunbe Kaur
Chan Chooi Man
Chan Mayin
Chan Ngai Chi
Chan Ngai Tim
Chan Ro Hong
Chan Saadon, Lynette
Chan Thiam Hwo
Chan Yoke Fun
Chang Yii Tan
Charles, Ravi
Cheah Suan Kee, Judy
Cheah Yoke Mooi
Chee Yu Chow
Cheong Wye Choon
Chew Leng Choo
Chew Poh Lee
Chew Poh Leng, Cherlene
Chew Thean Yean
Chew Wi Seng, Francis

Chi Teck Cheng
Chim Wai Main
Chin Kim Fook
Chin Shin Mun
Chin Sock Ee
Chin Wai Hin
Chin Yew Choong
Chin Yoke Mei
Chong Beng Suan
Chong Chow Yang
Chong Eng Li
Chong Hee Nam, Mike
Chong Sai Kin
Chong Teck Onn
Chong Wai Mei, Betty
Choo Sin Khuan, Simon
Choong Chan Sin
Choong Cheng Leng
Choong Foong Fei
Choong Kum Hoong
Choong Kwee Lan
Chow Kit Fai, Patrick
Chow Soo Fong
Chow, Pinky
Chua, Eddie
Chun Pik Kwan
Cubitt, Gerald
Cubitt, Janet
Dalbir Singh
Dawn, John David
Dekkers, Augustinus Josephus
Dennis Yong
Devathasan Apnair
Downes, Jan
E. Anis Malek
Eng Kwan Hai
Eng, Evelyn
Esbensen, Victor
Faizah Hj Ahmad Jamal
Fang Lee Har
Finney, Angus
Floer, Peter
Fong Yok King
Foo Poon Khean
Foong Seong Chee, Alex
Fox, Judy
Froggart, Paula
Gathercole, Peter J.
Gnanambikai Sabapathy
Goh Bee Lay, Winnie
Goh Chong Hin
Goh Haun Chuan
Goh Kiow Leng, Hedy
Goh Seng Aun
Goh Soah Hee
Goulding, Timothy
Graichen, Jayshree
Graichen, Victor

Guelden, Marlane
Hamizad Hashim
Hamsah Samsuddin
Han Li Chin
Harban Singh
Harbans Kaur
Hay, Valerie
Heah Hock Heng
Heng Kwee Lan, Jasmine
Hew Tze Yin
Hew Yoon Loong
Ho Lai Yoong
Ho Yueh Liang, Ivan
Ho Yuek Ming
Hoe Fong Sew
Hoffman. P
Horan Joanne
Hue Yoon Keong
Ibrahim Bajunid
Ibrahim Edham Hj Mohidin
Idris Marzuki
Ismail Salleh
Jalaludin Mat Jan
Jamaluddin Basharuddin
Jamil Misbah
Jamilah Osman
Jamri Tohid
Jayanthi Karen Sockalingam
Jayprakash Pertabai
Johan
Johari Mohd. Yusof
Junan Taib
K. Singaravelu
Kamaralzaman
Kan Kheong Thoo
Kanagaratnam, Patrick
Kanda Kumar
Khairul Anuar B Saidin
Khong Yin Swan
Khoo Fui Guat
Khoo Khay Heong
Khoo Soo Wan
Khoo Su Ming
Khor Siew Moi
Klahn, Jeffrey Eugene
Koh Weng Chuan, Brian
Koh, Colleen
Kok Kee Tat
Kok Swee Kheng
Kok Swee Ngor
Kun Yoke Pheng
Lai Chin Luke
Lai Mun Wai, Rodney
Lee Cheng Kin
Lee Choi Peng
Lee Khim Meng
Lee Kok Soon

Lee Kok Yuen
Lee Lai Choo
Lee Ling Kong
Lee Oon Teik
Lee Seng Piat
Lee Seong San
Lee Soon Fatt
Lee Su Win
Lee Tzu Hong
Lee Wei Yin
Leevers, Sarah Jane
Leong Boon Koon, Christine
Leong Choo Kong
Leong Kwok Peng
Leong Shown Chong
Leong Wai Seng, James
Leong, Pauline
Leow Kon Fah
Letchimee Devee
Lian Kam Pee
Liew Kim Seng
Liew Siew Lan
Lim Aun Tiah
Lim Chai See, Lucy
Lim Cham Gee
Lim Keng Kee
Lim Kim Chuan
Lim Kim Chye
Lim Kim Kee
Lim Kim Seng
Lim Lee Hock
Lim Paik Hong, Corene
Lim Poh Ann
Lim Swee Im
Lim Tean Bee
Lim Yee Meng
Lim, Isabel
Lim, Susan
Limann, Dirk
Liu Saow Hong
Liung Soo Hoong
Liyu Tuck Fatt
Loh Chi Leong
Loh Koh Leong, Daniel
Loh Mei Chin, Christine
Loh Seng Yee
Loh, Andrew
Loh, Patricia
Loh, Wilson
Lokeswary Sabapathipillay
Lonergan, Stephen
Long Chay Suang, Philip
Loo Wan Yong
Loo, Randy
Looi Wai Nam, William
Low Chai Kong
Low Chee Min
Low Kim Hong

Lum Wai Leng
Lum, Simon
M. Mooruthy
Maganjeet Kaur
Mahmud Abu
Makayu Soh
Malar Subramaniam
Maliza Sinniah
Maria Ambuvirayan
Martinez, Margaret Rose
Masrimie @ Rahim Yassim
Masrom Hasran
Masron Hasran
Md Nor Hassan
Md Yusof Mohd Pilus
Mishiyah Kalman
Misliyah Katman
Mohan Namasivayam
Mohan Ramanujam
Mohd Yassin Tan
Mohd Hanifah Yahaya
Mohd Kiruan Tasreju
Mohd Nasir Maidin
Mohd Saadon Latif
Mohd Yahya Mohd Sulaiman
Mohd Yusof Shari
Mohd. Ali Ismail
Mohd. Harun
Mohd. Hj. Said
Mohd. Rosli Mahmood
Mohd. Zullfeizan Manap
Moore, Wendy
Morais, Anne
Moran, Peter
Murphy, Joan
Mustapha Datah
Mustapha Mohamad
N Krishnasamy
Narayan Rao
Nasir Maidin
Ng Chee Meng
Ng Guat Leh, Sandra
Ng Tong San
Ngim, Rexon
Ngooi Ngok San
Nik Latifah Nik Salim
Nik Mohd. Nik Abd. Majid
Noorshah Hussin
Noorshinah Hussin
Noorminah Hussin
Norhara Hussein
Norhayati Mustapha
Norkamaruddin Aminallah
Norlia Saleh
Nowall, Lennart
Ong Guan Leong
Ong Kean Tong
Ong Soon Chye

Ooi Chwee Hoon
Ooi Soo Hock, Henry
Oon Kin Beng, Geoffrey
Oon Lai Kuen, Christine
Pak Kok Hong
Paling Sow
Peh Teong Khong
Phuan Kok Joo
Poh Gim Siew, Jackie
Poh Shaik Kiang
Poh Soon Pin
Ponniah, Carole Ann
Prema Pathumanathan
Purachal, John George
Pusparani
Puziah Jasman
Quah Wui Kiang, Lawrence
R. Rajanathan
Radzuan Mohd. Yusof
Rahimatsah Amat
Raich, James William
Rajinder Singh
Rama Rao
Ramachandran Ponnusamy
Ranjit Kaur Dhillon
Rasiah Mohd Mahbub
Razali Abd. Ghani
Razali Baki
Renganathan
Ripin Hj Senin
Robertson, John
Roggeman, Geert
Rohani Jelani
Rokiah Awang
Rosanor Abdu Ghani
Roslan Md Yusof
Rosli Assad
Rosna Ayub
Rosna Taib
Rozanor Abdul Ghani
Rubeli, Ken
S. Rajamanickam
Sabri John Arshad
Safii Hussain
Saiful Yazan Zulkifli
Saimas Ariffin
Salasilah Hassan
Salleh Ismail
Samari Hj. Hohd. Senang
Savarimuthu, Anthony
Saw Gek Hiock
Saw Swee Leng
Sazalee Abd Wahab
Scott, Eileen
Seah Po Choon
Seto Wai Ling, Danielle
Shaharin Yussof

Shahrir Abdul Samad, Datuk
Shaik Abbas Ibrahim
Shamini Dias
Shamsul Bahamin Mutalib
Sharp, Ilsa
Simon, Thomas
Siow Siew Eng
Siti Hawa Yatim
Sivaloganathan
Soo Kok Cheong
Soo Lye Hock
Strange, Morten
Subaraj Rajathurai
Sulaiman Esa
Sutari Supari
Syed Nurlhaq
Sze Tho Yow Yuan
Tajul Arus Kamaluddin
Tan Ah Tee
Tan Beng Ewe
Tan Chee Liang
Tan Cheng Li
Tan Chern Yin, Joseph
Tan Chi Seng
Tan Choo Guan
Tan Hoe Ang
Tan Hwai Chin
Tan Jiew Hoe
Tan Jooi Chong
Tan Kin Cheong
Tan King Pheow
Tan Lam Soon
Tan Liam Chwee
Tan Lita
Tan Siew Ching
Tan Teck Koon
Tan Tung Sim, Serena
Tan V.K., Vincent
Tan, Jackie
Tay Swee Leng, Irene
Tay, James
Tee Ming Huei
Tee Suai Kee
Tee, Robert Elok
Teh Eng Yow
Teh Eng Pin
Teh Ki Eng
Teh Kim Hong
Teh Lai Huat
Teh Thiam Oun
Teh Yew Kiang
Teng, David
Teo Hock Siong
Tho Lye Mun
Tho Lye Wye
Thoe Siew Lin, Jacqueline
Tian Yee Cheong
Tiang Siew Eng

Tong Yeoh Seng
Toy, Robin
Toy, Sandy
Tunku Mohd Nazim Yaacob
Turner, Ian Mark
V.N. Balasingam
Veer Jung Bharat
Wairah Marzuki
Walker, Daniel Arthur
Wan Adnan Wan Ismail
Wan Kamaruddin Ali
Wan Musa Wan Daud
Wan Zakiah Wan Omar
Wang Chih Fong
Waters, Brian
Waters, Marjorie
Wee Choo Chin
Wong Choo Ching
Wong Choong Hay
Wong Hoe Yeng, Richard
Wong Ju Kuan
Wong Kahoe
Wong Lai Keen
Wong M. C. May
Wong May Syn
Wong Mei Lin
Wong Poh Keng
Wong Tong Chow
Wong Woy Chun
Wong Young Soon
Wong Young Tseng
Wong Yuen Foo
Wong, Jackie
Wong, Kay
Wong, Martin
Woo Lee Pin
Woon Foo Khuen
Woon Tein Tet
Yap Hock Guan
Yap Peng Yan
Yap, Anthony
Yeap Soon Pin
Yeo Teng Hong
Yeo Tiang Chye
Yeoh Su Mei
Yeong Shoot Kian
Yin Ee Kok
Yin Khuat Seong, Paul
Yong Chan Chin
Yong Choong Choy
Yong Siew Kee, Frank
Yong Su Ha
Yong, Gwen
Young, Harry
Yuan Wee Ei
Yue Kham Wah
Zahary Mohd Kassim
Zain Ariffin Alkhadir

Zainab Wahidin
Zainal Abidin Abu Bakar
Zainal Abidin Sharif
Zainol Md Sharif
Zainuddin Abdul Rahim
Zainudin Baatu
Zubaid Akbar Neuleta Ahmad
Zuraida Abdullah
Zuriah Aljeffri
de Jong, Johnny
de Silva, Edda
de Silva, Faisal
de Silva, George
de Silva, Hafidz
der Meulen-Rijshouwe, Francesca

UNIVERSITY OF MALAYA

Abdul Aziz Ahmad Shah
Ahmad Makmur Hj Abdullah
Ahmad Salihin Mat Saat
Azman Mohd Nor
Che Mashim Tajuddin
Chen Hin Keong
Dayang Sadiah Abang Bohan
Dzulkarnain Mohamed
Edah Mohd Aris
Gabriel, Elizabeth P.
Hanili Ghazali
Isa Omar
Khairun Nisa Mohd Ramly
Mahmud Sider
Mazlan Mahli Hj Lamat
Maznah Kanji
Mohd Jamil Abdul Samad
Mohd Redzuan Omar
Mohd Sukri Yaakub
Mohd Taufik Abdul Ghani
Noliah Bakar
Noorazam Mohd Yusof
Noorizan Mior Nazri
Nur Aidah Ahmad Mansur
Pauzan Keat Wi
Razali Redzuan
Roshadah Hashim
Roslan Mohd Isa
Rusyatimah Tarimin
Sabariah Basir
Siti Rubiah Zainuddin
Tajudin Salim
Tohaini Osman
Wan Ab Rahim W Idris
Zaharah Hj Selamat
Zahratol Amani Hj Shahabuddin
Zainal Ariffin Mohd Isa
Zamari Mohd Ramli
Zohara Jamail
Zuriah Azmi

UNIVERSITI PERTANIAN MALAYSIA

Abd. Aziz Abd. Rahman
Abdul Rahim Mudin
Ahmad Zaini Zainuddin
Ayob Ahmadi
Hashim Md. Shari
Jasin Md. Yusof
Khairul Annuar Mat Supi
Makhdir Mardan
Noor Azhar Zainal
Ramlah Abu Bakar
Raup Meon
Ridzuan Mohd. Din

UNIVERSITI KEBANGSAAN MALAYSIA

Abd Rahim Abd Rahman
Abdullah Jusoh
Ahmad Feisal Mohd Kamil
Ahmad Rosdi Ahmad Idrus
Asogan Arumugam
Dahlina Daud Mahmud Lubin
Engku Muda Engku Musa
Fernandez, Jerald
Hafizah Kassim
Hishamuddin Hj Mohd
Holloway, Jude Stephen
Jaffry Ibrahim
Mahmud Sudin
Mathiuaanan Kalathurai
Mohd Nor Ramlan
Mohd Rafiq Norsham
Muhammad Halidin Das
Mustafah Md Nor
Norman Kamarudin
Pechdau Tohmeena
Ruslan Md Yusof
Tuan Hj Marzuki Tuan Yaakob
Zainudin Sumadi
Zalina Ibrahim
Zamry Mahput

INSTITUT TEKNOLOGI MARA

Abdul Malek Jaafar
Abdul Pilus Bharuddin
Ahmad Kambali Khalil
Annuar Mohd Yaacob
Ashari Abd Jalil
Hamdan Selaman
Mohd Jalil Ayub
Mohd Khairi Abd Karim

Mohd Noor Zurimi
Mohd Shuhaimi Wan Azel
Mohd Tamizi Mustafa
Mohd Zukhi Omar
Norniza Ithnin
Ridzuan Ramli
Rosaidan Latip
Shahron Sharuddin
Syed Abu Bakar Syed Hamzah
Zaini Ithnin Hj Razak
Zanariah Mohd Arifin

MARA, Melaka

Ahmad Yusri Yussoff
Azhar Yusof
Esah Manap
Faridah Deraman
Fatimah Mohd. Sidek
Razam Mohd. Rashid

MARA, Taiping

Fauzi Zakaria
Halim Mohd. Sohod
Md. Azmi Karnain
Mohd. Ferdius Abd. Kadir
Mohd. Hashim Jumaat
Mohd. Maznihan Mohd. Nor
Sahwan Salim

MARA, Kota Bahru

Abdul Rahim An
Ahmad Filza Ismail
Ahmad Zaki Rahman
Bidi Abdul Hamid
Che Mat Derasid
Jusoh Awang Semili
Mazlan Filza Ismail
Mohd. Zaidi Hasan

MARA, Kuantan

Abdullah Wahab
Azmir Adzhar
Halim Hitam
Md. Daut Md. Mara
Md. Qamari
Ridzuan Ramli
Shamsul Ismail
Tengku Zulkarni

MARA, Negri Sembilan

Abdul Rahim Mat Pilus
Ahmad Nazir Lateh
Ismail Hashim

Kamarulzaman Mohd. Nasir
Misna Annuar Abdul Hadi
Mohd. Khatta Daem
Mohd. Zamzuri Mohd. Hassan
Muhammad Hazlaum Ibrahim
Zulkifli Hashim

MARA, Kedah

Ahmad Nazri Mohd. Nozin
Ahmad Zaid Abdul Hamid
Kamaralzaman Md. Ali
Mohd. Rashid Zainal Abidin
Mohd. Yusof Mohd. Isahali
Muhammad Kamaruddin
Shaiful Azmi Yahya
Wan Ahmad Ariffin

MARA, Pulau Pinang

Abdul Halim Mohd.
Abdul Rahman Ahmad
Badrol Hisam Abdul Ralip
Mohd. Wijan Zaini
Muzaffar Mazlan
Zalizan Kassim
Zamri Yusoff
Zulkifli Kassim

NATIONAL UNIVERSITY OF SINGAPORE

Abdul Hakim Mohd. Ismail
Chee Chye Yeen
Chee May Shan, Vivien
Chew, Annie
Chua Sook Lian
Gunasekara, Dunbara Santie
Howe Choon Hong, Matthew
Khoo Kuan Liang, Grey
Koh Mei Choo, Adeline
Lim Guat Hong
Lim Hock Eng
Lim Hock Heong, Christopher
Lim Malin
Lim Yuan Tuck
Loo Eng Hock
Mathiyalargan Krishnan
Rao, Anishesarppe Narayan
Samsuri
Shu Choo Ching, Wendy
Tan Tiong Wah, Hugh
Ting Saw Kheng, Angeline
Toh Chwee Lian, Adeline
Wee Yeow Chin
Wong Pek Foong

UNITED WORLD COLLEGE, Singapore

Bennion, Matthew John
Binding, Rebecca Louise
Bird, Lara
Carter, Pamela Marion
Foxlee, Brendan John
Goh Kuo-Liang, Thomas Jeremy
Heres, Jacob Cornelius
Hill, Jeremy Noel
Kelly, Jennifer Lisa
Kelly, Kenneth Jeffrey
Lee Toun, Greg
MacCallum, Peter James
Page, Hilary Jean
Page, John Dennis
Peterson, Katherine Lee
Pickford, Shirley
Sandison, Tracylee
Short, Katherine
Smith, Brendan Ian
Smith, Helen
Tunnacliffe, Victoria
Van Oord, Govert
Westerhoek, Ekke-Jan
Zagrodnika, Stefanie

STAR PUBLICATIONS (M) BHD.

Fong Ten Chee
Ho, Jimmy
Kee, Irene
Liew Peng Chuan
Loo Wai Tong
Low Eng Sim
Ngiam Pick Ngoh, Linda
Ng Kok Wah
Ng Poh Tip
Ng Yew Choy
Tan Chee Keong, William
Tan Gim Ean
Wee, Margaret
Yeong Soo Lan
Yong Shan Fook

HOUSING DEVELOPERS ASSOCIATION

Chin Too Nam
Chong, Peter
Lee Chew Loong, Kenneth
Lee Chu Keng
Lee Seaw Sin
Lee Yee Teng
Yew Ah Bean
Wong Hor Wai
Wong Nyan Ken

MALAYAN TOBACCO COMPANY SCHOLARS

Chang Keng Choong
Chiam Yow Fung
Chong Chee Koon, Thomas
Jamil Derus Ahmad
Kader Ridwan Hj Kader Ghouse
Lim Yew Siang
Loo Chi Woei
Mariam Mohd
Ng Kah Eng
Nooraini Othman
Rosmah Ismail
Salina Taib
Sethupathy, Joan
Sheikh Abbas
Sulaiman Yahya
Tan Chern Fung, Eugene
Tan Yew Luen
Veramohan Nadarajah
Wong Hee Pong
Wong Kim Lan
Wong Ong Choi
Yip Ting Wai, Richard

ARTISTS

Ahmad Azidi Amin
Ahmad Khalid Yusof
Chin Wan Kee
Choong Kam Kow
Hamidah Mohd. Noor
Ismail Hashim
Khalid Ibrahim
Khatijah Sanusi
Lim Eng Hooi
Mustapha Haji Ibrahim
Nurshansi Mohd. Noor
Sharifah Fatimah Syed Zubir
Sulaiman Hj. Esa
Syed Ahmad Jamal
Syed Nabil
Yeoh Jin Leng
Yong Chien Chin
Zainol Abidin Ahmad Shariff

TV3

Han Chong Huat
Haji Hashim Omar
Mohd. Pitry Aziz
Nasir Ismail
Nina Halim Rasip
Nortajuddin
Puthoraja Appalanaidu
Ramly Md. Noh

RTM

Tajaddin Ahmad
Wahab Umak
Yahya Sulaiman
Yusof Pilus

CATHOLIC HIGH SCHOOL,
Petaling Jaya

Beh Seng Tong
Cheng Shock Meng
Chin Chee Hing
Chin Siew Sern
Cho Kok Leong
Choo Lee Chow
Foong Hoe Meng
Kok Kuan Ki
Lai Chee Sing
Lim Meow Fook
M. Pasupathy
Pang Fui Yuen
Phang Siew Yang
Soo Chan Fai
Tan Yoke Ling
Thian Soong Yee
V. Pasupathy
Yong Kok Shing

CONVENT, Negri Sembilan

Chin Fook Meng, David
Chin Sik Ping, Jennifer
Chin Yee Kiong
David Fonseka, Shalinee
Foong Lie
Khoo Yew Suan, Ivy
Kok Chow Hioong
Lam Bee Theng
Maniam, Annie
Shanmuganathan, Sharmila

JOHOR SCHOOLS

Abd Razak Haron
Chong Kok Wei, David
Hashim Basir
Hishammudin Ahmad
Mohd Johari Ayob
Mohd Munawar Mohd Nazer
Mohd Sharifudin Mahmood
Mustapa Hj Ibrahim
Othman Ahmad
Roslie Mohamad
Soo Yieh Chon
Ungku Ahmad Zahrin

MAXWELL SCHOOL,
Kuala Lumpur

Tan Siew Mee
Foo Yat Chin
Tanuj Kumar
Adlan Rahim Omar
Shila Bai
Leong Kwee Sian
Lim Chin Kah
Cutter, Andrew Lancelot
Khong Weng Tuck

METHODIST GIRLS SCHOOL,
Kuala Lumpur

Chandra Kala
Chang Mei Ling
Chong Wai Ling
Komala
Loh Wai Yee
Low Bee Yin
Tan Bee Lin
Wong Ling Chee
Yap, Dilys
Yap Mei Ling

METHODIST ENGLISH SCHOOL,
Banting

Azman Samingam
Balasubramaniam Alagan
Ignatius Muscrinas
K. Salah Kulasingam
Lee Gin Kheng
Murali Krishnan Pavadaisamy
Samuel George s/o M.S. George
Saraswathy Balakaju
Shahoul Razi Omar
Syed Ahmad Zamri Syed Aziz
Thanapalan s/o Thagaraju

SEK. MEN. CHUNG HWA WEI SIN,
Terengganu

Chua Hock Guan
Chua Lian Beng
Gan Yen Ling
Guan Kok Yaw
Koh Jee Koan
Lee Meng Sin
Lim Yee Meng
Lua Peck Lay
Ong Bee Lin
Ong Chee Keong
Ong Fei Li, Joanne

Ong Suan Mei
Poh Boon Teng
Tan Bee Lai
Teo Chai Yaw
Wee Beng Tang
Wee Chung Lui

SEK. MEN. SEA PARK,
Petaling Jaya

Chin Fui See
Eow Khean Fatt
Gan Ghee Hoong, Simon
Goh Keat Leong
Koh Thian Hock
Koh, Augustine (Mrs)
Lee Chee Herng
Leong Yue Bing, Albert
Sin Biow Khoon, Ramona
Soh Tak Fatt
Ting Siew Hoong

SMJK JINJANG, Kuala Lumpur

Chin Hon Koon
Chong Choon Seng
Law Lai Huat
Law Siau Kian
Lew Kin Soon
Lian Lam Chuan
Liau Pooy Lan
Liew Chee Ming
Loong Kok Foong
Low Choo Chan
Low Meng Koon
Soo Lin Chai
Tan Cheng Teik
Tan Cher Buey
Tan You Tek

SMJK LA SALLE, Petaling Jaya

Devaganesan Rajoo
Khoo Boon Tsen, Terence
Ong, Shirley
Paul, Sean
Prince Guneratnam Jr.
Sangay a/l Ganaganayagam
Shahin al-Rashid
Sia Teng Leong
Soo Hong Wah, Edward
Suresh Chelliah
Tan Lee Swee Hin
Yim Mun Lee
Yong Kian Leong, Marcus

SMJK SERI GARING,
Banting

Cheah Lai Ying, Annie (Mrs)
Dharmarajah
Hew Meng Chin
Mong Choy Tieng
Oh Soan Ming
Rossimah Darus
Shakela M Segaran
Tan Ming Choo
Teoh Khiam Joo
Wong Kean Heng
Zaed Shaez

SMR KAHANG,
Kluang

Chin Siu Hi
Chong Wan Foo
Chow Chew Moy
Goh Chee Kwan
Kam Wee Heng
Kok Kim Hock
Lam Yoke Chiew
Leong Sew Keng
Lew Yoke Chin
Liow Kim Sin
Ng Sook Ling
Tan Chi Seng
Tan Yew Beng

VICTORIA INSTITUTION,
Kuala Lumpur

Arulsothy Ragunathan
Cheong Pak Meng
Chia Kok Fen
Chin Yeow Chong
Choy Kian Meng, Alan
Chua, Edward
Hoh Chee Kee
Iskandar Rauf Idris Rauf
Kong Shuih Huei
Lau Kah Pew
Lee Chor Onn
Lim Siew Fai
Loh Yet Hun
Mohd Ali Abu Bakar
Mohd. Annuar Abdul Hamid
Yap Boong Kah

Any errors and omissions are greatly regretted. Please inform Malayan Nature Society so that mistakes can be rectified in future editions.

The following are thanked for their invaluable co-operation and assistance:

Director-General, Forest Research Institute Malaysia
Director-General, Institute for Medical Research
Director-General, Malaysian Agricultural Research and
    Development Institute
Ibu Pejabat Jabatan Perlindungan Hidupan Liar dan
    Taman Negara (PERHILITAN)
Jabatan Angkatan Tentera
Jabatan Hal Ehwal Orang Asli, Cawangan Johor
Jabatan Perhutanan Negeri Johor
Jabatan Perlindungan Hidupan Liar dan Taman Negara,
    Negeri Johor
Jabatan Perlindungan Hidupan Liar dan Taman Negera,
    Negeri Pahang
Jawatankuasa Kerja Keselamatan Negeri Johor
Jawatankuasa Keselamatan Negeri Pahang
Kahang Police, Kahang Police Station
Leong Heng Nin, Dato
Malayan Nature Society, Johor Branch
Malayan Nature Society, Selangor Branch
Manager, Bukit Cantik Estate
Markas Group Gerakkhas Kem Pasifik
Markas Wilayah Udara Satu
Ng Chee Cheong, Dato
Pejabat Hutan Negeri Pahang
Pejabat Menteri Besar, Johor
Pejabat Menteri Besar, Kuantan
Pejabat Setiausaha Kerajaan, Negeri Johor
Pejabat Setiausaha Kerajaan Negeri Pahang
Phillip Kuok, Tan Sri
Radio Televisyen Malaysia
Sistem Televisyen Malaysia Berhad (TV3)
UNESCO-MAB
Unit Perancang Ekonomi Negeri Johor
Unit Perancang Ekonomi Negeri Pahang
Vice-Chancellor, Universiti Kebangsaan Malaysia
Vice-Chancellor, Universiti Malaya
Vice-Chancellor, Universiti Pertanian Malaysia
Vice-Chancellor, Universiti Sains Malaysia

MNS is grateful to all members and friends who
helped in one way or another during the expedition.

index

Scientific names of genera and species are given in italics. Page numbers in bold type refer to illustrations.

Geographical terms listed in Malay include Batu (rock); Bukit (hill); Gunung (mountain); Jeram (rapids); Kampung (village); Kuala (confluence); Padang (clearing); Pulau (island); and Sungai (river).